C0-APK-857

Praise for Sacred Seeds

"These well-written non-fiction stories offer a beautiful look at a childhood filled with love, learning and self-sufficiency. The collection shows how hard work, faith and family shaped a young girl into a bright, strong woman with a deeply held commitment to helping others. At times funny, poignant, exciting and mysterious, these 32 vignettes are windows to the past and hold subtle important lessons for living today. The author's experience is rural Northern New Mexico during the 1930s, but the themes ring universal."
– Anne Hillerman, *New York Times* best-selling author

"While the rest of America grappled with the economic wrath laid bare by the Great Depression, the Hispanic people of northern New Mexico faired far better because all they ever knew was poverty. Thousands of people were forced to leave their homes during this era, but the people of northern New Mexico stayed, firmly planted in the land of their ancestors. To an onlooker it appeared that they had little, but in reality, they had everything. Their unrelenting faith, traditions, songs, and most importantly, family, not only sustained them, but provided the determination to thrive. With *Sacred Seeds*, Mari-Luci Jaramillo has woven together the cultural fabric that is New Mexico."
– Ana Pacheco, author of eight books on New Mexican history

Sacred Seeds is "a wonderful story of a young girl's rich experiences in a rapidly disappearing way of life. Forcibly made Americans overnight, her grandparents were part of the last generation to live in the traditional way. Mari-Luci fully embraced the challenge and promise inherent in joining the larger American culture, where she became almost unimaginably successful. Still, she insists that her success grew from 'The sacred seeds of faith and community, of the passion for learning and the love of the land...' acquired at her grandparents *ranchito*."
– Doyle Daves, twice recipient of the Marc Simmons Award for Historic Writing

"*Sacred Seeds* is a MUST read: The foundation, details and cultural tones highlighted by the Honorable Mari Luci Jaramillo will fill you with love, warmth, and laughter...."
– Dr. Loui Olivas, President, American Association of Hispanics in Higher Education

"The Good Old Days . . . before telephones, television, internet, cars, planes, running water, electricity, Facebook, snapchat, and Instagram. How did children live, what did they do for fun? Join Mari-Luci as she retells her lived experiences growing up in her beloved Northern New Mexico on her *abuelos' ranchito* before becoming an ambassador was even a dream, let alone a reality. *Sacred Seeds* by Mari-Luci Jaramillo is a compelling story of love, family, resiliency, community, and the power of faith. The fundamental appeal is multi-faceted:

- For teenagers the age of Mari-Luci, her stories of growing up in New Mexico and the time spent on her grandparents' *ranchito* will be a journey into a different era;
- For teachers, the book will serve as a resource to bring history to life and help students reflect on their own lives and write their own stories;
- For readers who grew up in Northern New Mexico or similarly populated regions, it will be a reminder of times and lived experiences of a bygone era;
- For readers interested in learning about other cultures and other regions, it will provide insights into the rich bilingual and bicultural historical context of Northern New Mexico."

– JoAnn Canales, PhD, Professor, College of Education and Human Development, Texas A&M University-Corpus Christi

Sacred Seeds:
A Girl, her Abuelos, and the Heart of Northern New Mexico

by Mari-Luci Jaramillo
author of
Madame Ambassador: the Shoemaker's Daughter

with Cecilia J. Navarrete

BARRANCA PRESS

Copyright © 2019 by Mari-Luci Jaramillo.

All rights reserved. This book may not be reproduced in whole or in part, by any means (with the exception of short quotes for the purpose of review), without permission of the publisher. For information, address Barranca Press via editor@barrancapress.com.

Cover Landscape by Cecilia J. Navarrete. Illustrations by Cecilia J. Navarrete. Cover photo of the authors by Jim Estrada. Cover design by Dan Levine; text design by Wayne Banks.

First Edition: 2019

HC ISBN: 9781939604-347

PB ISBN: 9781939604-354

Library of Congress Control Number: 2019941577

Subject Areas:

YOUNG ADULT NONFICTION

Biography & Autobiography / Social Activists

Biography & Autobiography / Women

Biograph & Autobiography / US Ambassadors

People & Places / United States / Hispanic & Latino

United States / Southwest / New Mexico

English with Spanish.

Manufactured in the United States of America.

To my sister, Elvira Antuna de Romero, who was my inspiration for writing this book. Even though you are no longer with us, know that I love you, hermanita. These stories are for you and our shared memories.

And for my children and grandchildren, may you find inspiration and strength from my life experiences.

Mari-Luci Jaramillo

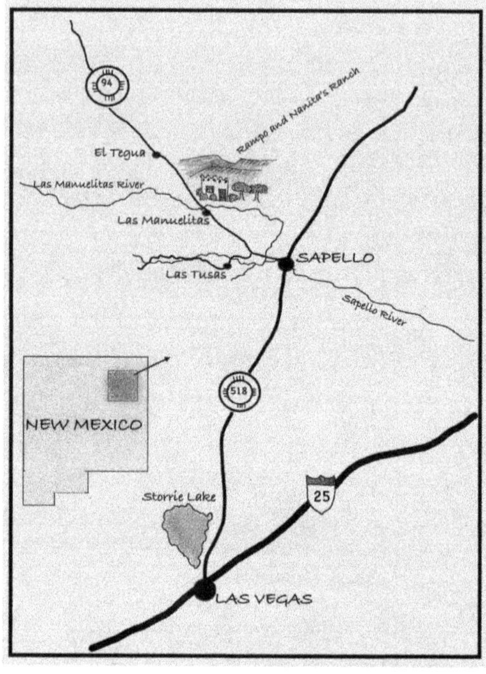

Table of Contents

Chapter 1: Where do I begin?

How could a girl from rural northern New Mexico who grew up in poverty, become the first Hispanic female ambassador of the United States? Reflecting on my childhood, I can remember the key moments that opened my eyes to the possible, to what would become my sacred seeds.

As a preteen, I was very shy. Yet, I couldn't help but ask the "why" of things. I bombarded everyone around me with questions. I only stopped when I was satisfied with the answers or when the person, out of sheer exhaustion, told me, "*No se.*" I don't know.

I heard "*no se*" often in our uneasy family home. My parents, Elvira Ruiz and Maurilio Antuna, were opposites and the tension between them left little room for their curious child. Although Papito was handsome and a brilliant self-educated man, he was always busy with "his" work of music and leather crafting. He was seldom home. Mamita, like most Hispanic women of her day, stayed home to care for the household. Her beauty, good cooking, and pious ways did nothing to keep Papito home. Mamita accepted her unhappy marriage with dignity and focused on ways to nurture her children.

Their first child was named Elvira. Vera was an only child until I arrived seven years later. My brother, Maurilio Jr., known as Junior, joined us two years after my birth. Mamita's ultimate dream was for the three of us to succeed in school. She constantly reminded us that education would be the ticket out of poverty, free us from being dependent on anyone, and allow us to make our own choices. But how was I going to get an education if everyone kept telling me, *"no se"*?

Little did I know that Silviano Tafoya and Juanita Ruiz Tafoya would be the two people in my life to open the doors of learning about the possible and to help me find the answers to my questions about the world. We called Silviano and Juanita our *abuelos*, our grandparents, but they were actually our aunt and uncle. When Mamita was born, her mother had three other young daughters to raise and was too ill after giving birth to care for another child. The only alternative she had was to give her baby to someone she could trust. That person turned out to be her eldest daughter, Juanita Ruiz, who at age eighteen married twenty-year-old Silviano Tafoya. Silviano and Juanita were childless for two years after their marriage and happily adopted Mamita as their own precious child.

Grandpa Silviano, who we nicknamed Rampo, was self-educated and well respected by his entire community. He had a love for learning that he freely shared with his "grandchildren". Grandma Juanita, whose name we shortened to Nanita, was a tiny whirlwind and expert on everything in her home and on their *ranchito*.

Others involved in my young close-knit world of wonder included Vera and Junior. Although we were born several years apart, the three of us were very close and shared many experiences. The last group of people to round out my education were people cultivated by my grandparents. They were known as *comadres* and *compadres*, godmothers and godfathers, or very close friends.

For more details about each of the people in my life, see "Mi Gran Familia" and "Family Photographs."

The events from my childhood that I share in this book occurred not too long after my grandparents bought land to establish their ranch south of Mora in the village of Las Manuelitas, New Mexico. The *ranchito* actually was a combination of a farm and a ranch. It was composed of a small house, a barn, a tack room for storing tools and equipment, a corral, and a few acres for growing crops and fruit trees, as well as a cow, two horses, and several chickens.

While somewhat isolated, Las Manuelitas was not far from other small settlements. To the north was El Tegua and to the south was Las Tusas. Each village consisted of a small collection of *ranchos*. To the east of Las Manuelitas was El Sapelló, which was located near the main highway. It had a post office, a church, a grocery store, and a dance hall.

Many of these *ranchos* were established around the 18th century by Spanish settlers. Due to their isolation, the faith and way of life of these Spanish-speaking families changed very little under the rule of Spain and later Mexico. But when their lands were handed over to the United States in 1912 and New Mexico became the 47th state, the villagers found themselves having to learn a new language and culture. As a result of this history, my *abuelos* and Mamita spoke a variant of sixteenth and seventeenth century Spanish.

By the 1920s, opportunity boomed in the bustling village of Las Vegas, New Mexico not far from the ranching communities. Papito dreamed of careers as a shoemaker and musician. So, in the land of lush green *vegas*, big trees and bigger dreams, my parents made Las Vegas their home.

We siblings were born in Las Vegas just before and during the Great Depression when life changed for everyone. The economy tumbled across the entire nation, but it seemed especially bad in our immediate surroundings. Few had money to purchase what Papito had to offer in the village. The price of crops and livestock dropped so low that some ranchers had to sell their land and move away to find work.

To add to the difficulties for those who stayed, rich landowners from the north began to dam the rivers, which reduced water flow into our community creeks and rivers. Having little water resulted in poorer crops and little success at subsistence living.

We also experienced a long drought, known as the Dust Bowl period of 1931-1935. During these difficult times, trading became a way of life, as few people had money to buy the items they needed. Food items that could not be grown by the ranchers, like flour, sugar, and cinnamon, were bought on credit from the local grocery *patrón* in Sapelló.

For extra money, men traveled out-of-state to pick crops at harvest time in Colorado or Texas and left their wives to maintain the ranches. The men returned with cash for their hard work, but only made enough to pay the grocer and open a new credit account for the following year. These were very tough times, and we all lived on the edge of extreme poverty.

My memories are of these harsh, but amazing, community experiences. In *Sacred Seeds*, I write in English, the language of my formal education, but also use my grandparents' and Mamita's archaic Spanish, as well as Papito's standard Mexican Spanish. *Sacred Seeds* are the values of education, faith, love, community, dignity, and respect that were instilled in us and that made it possible for my siblings and me to escape poverty as successful and literate bilingual professionals.

Escape to my Happy Place

Chapter 2: Journey to Paradise

We never knew how we were going to get there.

It did not matter to me. The sun was rising over the high plains east of Las Vegas, New Mexico, and I could not wait to get started. I quietly dressed and sat on my bed, reading. Mamita finally came into our room and whispered to us that it was time to make the twelve mile journey to our *abuelos' ranchito* in Las Manuelitas.

Occasionally, Papito would take us in his car. It was his car, not the family car. He used it for work and rarely let us ride with him. Leading an almost separate life from us, we never knew if he would sleep at his shoe shop, where he kept a bed, or come home late at night and sleep until noon. Mamita accepted this strained relationship to keep peace in the house and so did we. That is the way it was in those days. However, my mother never waited for Papito to take us to visit Rampo and Nanita.

On the weekends, when there was nice weather, Mamita and us kids would walk the distance to the *ranchito*. We left early Saturday morning and returned late Sunday afternoon. During the summer and on holidays, she allowed us to take turns and spend longer periods with our *abuelos*. I guess three kids were too many for them to handle at once.

We typically started our journey by leaving our house on Second Street and walking toward Seventh Street, which led north and out of town. Once out of Las Vegas, we would take a shortcut across fields filled with tall weeds. I would hold my breath every time we walked across the field and tried not to shout out in pain. Those weeds harbored lots of bugs, caterpillars, and flying insects. It was extra bad for Mamita and us girls because in those days tradition did not allow us to wear pants, and the bugs took advantage of our exposed legs. I always left those fields full of bites.

About a third of the way, we would pass Storrie Lake. This beautiful lake had an island in the middle. Every time we walked by the lake, I asked Mamita if I could learn to swim, so I could go and stand on the island. We did not have any pools in Las Vegas and Mamita did not know how to swim, but she was always positive and would assure me that one day it would be possible, saying, *"Algún día, míja."*

Once past the lake, we walked on a gravel road. When cars drove by, we had to duck the rocks and pebbles that the cars kicked up. The gravel road continued north, winding around low hills until it reached the top of a slope called the "Nine-Mile Hill." The hill was really a *mesa* and was nine miles from our village of Las Vegas.

I was always tired by then, but never complained once we got to the top. The vegetation was completely different at this altitude. As far as we could see, there were wide fields of grass speckled with low scrub oak, all of which was enveloped by big blue skies and soaring clouds. To the west, jutting high in the sky was our beautiful and majestic Hermit's Peak. Many said that Hermit's Peak was named long ago after Giovanni Maria de Agostini who we called *El Santo Padre.* The legend we had learned was that this Holy Father was an Italian monk who lived alone in a cave up on the mountain. While he devoted his life to solitude, he was known as a healer and the local people would go to him when sick.

Even though Hermit's Peak distracted me from our walk, my mind drifted back to how hard it was going to be to climb the upcoming *mesa*. It was at this point that I prayed for a ride. Sometimes, Rampo and Nanita would drive down to meet us just before we had to climb what we called Nine-Mile Hill. After so many weekend visits, they must have figured out when to meet us in their black Model A Ford with a two-person rumble seat. We all wanted to ride in that back seat and let the wind blow through our hair! The three of us kids would squabble until Rampo decided who would ride in back going to the *ranchito* and who would ride there on the return trip.

When we reached thc top of the *mesa*, Rampo would pull over and stop for a few minutes so we could pray at the *descanso.* This rest stop was a place where several local people had died in a car crash and where their relatives placed crosses as a memorial. As the car came to a halt, Rampo would remove his hat and wipe his brow. That was the signal for everyone, including him, to get out of the car and kneel in front of the *descanso.* He would lead us in prayer, thanking God for being so good to us and keeping us together as a family. We also prayed for all those who had been killed on that road, praying that their souls were in heaven. Nanita would then lead us in singing a few holy *cánticos* or *canciones* such as:

Bendito, bendito, ¡bendito sea Dios!
Los ángeles cantan y alaban a Dios.
Los ángeles cantan y alaban a Dios.
Yo creo, Jesús mío, que estás en el altar.
Oculto en la Hostia, te vengo a adorar.
Oculto en la Hostia, te vengo a adorar.

Blessed, blessed, blessed be God!
The angels sing and praise God.
The angels sing and praise God.
I believe, my Jesus, that you are at the altar.
Hidden in the Host, I come to worship you.
Hidden in the Host, I come to worship you.

After our prayers and songs, we would drink water from a big glass jar that my *abuelos* always carried and sometimes they gave us crackers and even a small candy or two. On occasion, the entire group shared a penny packet of Red Hots, a tiny cinnamon candy that I loved. After the treat, we would climb back into the car until the next stop. Not too far away, was the tiny village of Sapelló where Rampo would stop at the grocery store. It was here that Rampo would buy his usual two gallons of gasoline. As he came back to the car, Rampo would say to Nanita, "*Les compré dulces de cubeta.*" The storekeeper kept a variety of hard candies in *cubetas*. His customers would scoop candies out of these buckets and into small paper bags. Our hands would immediately stretch straight out for Nanita to parcel out the candy like a mother bird sharing with her *pajaritos* opening their beaks to be fed.

After our stop at the grocery store, we turned toward the west on an even narrower dirt road to cross the Sapelló River on a wooden one-lane bridge. Only one car could pass at a time – carefully and slowly!

When our *abuelos* were not able to pick us up, we had to walk to their house from Sapelló. Mamita let us walk under the bridge and step into the cool clear water of the meandering stream. She would tell us, *"Pueden jugar en el agua, pero tienen que quitarse los zapatos y colgarlos alrededor de sus cuellos. Y, no los dejen caer en el agua."* That was Mamita's rule: we could enjoy putting our bare feet in the water if we kept our shoes dry by tying them around our necks.

After crossing, we shook our feet dry, put on our socks and shoes, and continued, a little cooler, up the slight hill to the tiny community of Las Tusas. The homes here were made of reddish rock and beautiful crimson plastered adobes. From whatever angle you looked, the houses had a reddish hue.

The narrow dirt road had lots of big ruts, sometimes as much as a foot deep. Every time it rained or snowed, the road was impassable until it dried a few days later. The neighbors would then bring their teams of horses to level it again with an attached *escrepa*. In the winter it was a beautiful scene, with the red dirt and the contrasting white snow. When a few cars tried to go through the gooey mess, they would squirt red mud onto the white snow and create incredible images. I'm sure the drivers who tried to escape the clutches of that mud saw nothing beautiful about it, but I loved the designs of Mother Earth.

As we passed the small assemblage of Las Tusas family homes, we would turn slightly northeast and cross a dangerous *arroyo* that was sometimes dry and sometimes treacherous after a heavy rain or when the snow melted. Many times, in both summer and winter, Rampo's car would get stuck and we all had to get down to push the car out of the mud-sucking ruts. Nanita would pray in a loud voice, *"San Antonito, sácanos de estos aprietos."* It seemed that Saint Anthony answered Nanita's prayers through Rampo, who cut large pine branches from surrounding trees and laid heavy stones on them to get the car out of the mud.

The slipping and sliding were not just something the car did. We kids got into the act too. We soon found ourselves falling on our knees when pushing the car and rolling in the muck. By the time it was over, we were covered in mud. Nanita and Mamita would make the sign of the cross, gently scold us, and with some effort scrape off as much mud as they could before allowing us back into the car.

Sometimes our compadres would come along on their horses and get down to help dislodge us from the gooey mess. I always thought it was funny when they arrived and greeted us by saying, *"Buenas tardes. ¿Qué se atascaron?"* Couldn't they see we were stuck? Nanita said to never to make fun of *los mayores*, so I never did get to ask the adults why they would state the obvious. Instead, we politely returned the greeting and affirmed that we were stuck.

After getting out of the gully and up the next winding hill, we had a nice straight road for a couple of miles. Finally, we came to a gate that marked the entrance boundary of my *abuelos'* land. Regardless of whether we were walking or riding in the car, we kids would argue as to whose turn it was to open the barbed-wire gate. It was not easy, but we loved to do it. The gate consisted of four or five skinny poles standing straight up and holding the strands of barbed wire taut. We would unlatch the wire loop that held the gate up to the main fence post. We then pulled the gate away from the road, so everyone could pass through. We always felt so grown up that we could open the gate. It took some strength to get it done, a true demonstration of our growing into adulthood. I loved it when we could say that we had opened the gate, *"Podíamos abrir la puerta."*

Beyond the gate, we could see two mountain ridges rise on either side of us as we drove or walked through a huge open space planted on both sides of the narrow road with crops such as pinto beans that only need a little rain. We followed the straight, dusty road until it ended at the edge of Las Manuelitas Creek. We then had to open another gate and ford the rocky river to the other side. Because floods would prevent us from crossing, Rampo built a very high, narrow foot-bridge that was made with ropes, wires, bolts, nuts, and boards. For fear that we would fall, my *abuelos* always yelled, *"Cuidado, no se vayan a caer."* Nanita would add in her northern New Mexico Spanish, *"Deténganse del cabresto,"* insisting that we hold on to the rope.

We had lots of fun on that bridge when grownups were not around. Playing on the footbridge was like being in a jungle movie. When severe flooding tore the bridge away from its posts, we would have to walk across the river in the murky water. We never knew what we might encounter. Concealed branches might scratch our legs. Buried boulders torn from the sides of the river might make us lose our balance and fall. Floating uprooted trees might grab at us and take us down the stream. We needed all our senses to navigate safely across the river.

For our parents and *abuelos*, the brown surging water signaled exhausting work ahead. Rampo would say, *"Qué belleza, ni belleza...Esto es puro trabajo."* Whether they were beautiful or not, the waters indicated hard work ahead.

And he was right. They had to move the big boulders that blocked cars from driving across the river. They also had to fix the torn walking bridge and repair the dirt walls they had built to protect their crops. You would think that everyone would be overwhelmed with all they had to do in addition to the daily chores, but no. My family knew that the mountains were receiving much needed water and that water was being shared with them. Our *abuelos* would pray, *"Gracias Señor, por la destrucción mínima, y sin embargo, dándonos agua que tanto necesitamos."* Thank you, Lord, they prayed, for keeping the destruction down and yet providing them with much needed water. Like everything else in their lives, they were thankful to God for whatever they possessed.

Regardless of the conditions, once we crossed the river, there was only a short ride or walk up the narrow dirt road to our *abuelos'* home. Even if we had a ride, usually we chose to walk or run this section of the journey. On the right side of the road, there was a deep well that my *abuelos* had dug, so we stopped for a quick drink. In the well was a pump where we could get water, but we had to prime the pump first. We did this by pushing the big handle up and down until a gush of cool water would come out and splash us. After taking delight in the well, we ran up the road that was now surrounded by beautiful apple orchards. If there were apples on the trees, we stopped to help ourselves. If the trees were bare, we ran wild, chasing each other amongst the trees and yelling with glee.

We would keep running and cross the huge wooden planks that formed a bridge over the wide ditch that went by the front part of the house. Along the way to the house was a vegetable garden where we knew Rampo or Nanita would soon bring us to pull up delicious carrots, to cut cucumbers, and to gather green peas.

We now could see our *abuelos* waving to us from their big front porch. Their home stood on the hillside of the property and they could see the main road, fields, river, and ditches that crossed their property. We would run faster when we were close to the house, fly up the steps onto the huge porch, and leap into our *abuelos'* arms. The good times were about to begin.

In our rush to be in the arms of our *abuelos*, we would leave Mamita behind. Rampo would gently remind us to go back and bring her to the house. When we returned, three or four minutes later, we were rewarded with big glasses of cool herbal tea or sometimes even Kool Aid with the traditional New Mexico *biscochitos*. Those cookies were the best.

We had arrived. We were finally in a real home.

Chapter 3: The Place We Called Home

Our *abuelos* always welcomed our help at the *ranchito*.

The ranch was small, but constantly needed work. I did not mind helping. Actually, I looked forward to the daily chores.

Part of the magic of helping was Nanita's praise for my efforts. I could always count on her saying, "*Mijita, que buena trabajadora eres. Barres muy bien.*" She praised me as a good worker even for doing a simple job such as sweeping. She said this phrase every time I used her trusty hand-made weed broom to sweep the large patio with small, evenly spaced strokes. When I sprinkled water from a bucket to keep the dust down, the dirt smelled like fresh rain from heaven. Once done, the whole area looked as if no one had ever stepped on it. Neither a leaf nor a stone marred the brown beauty. All along the edges, I raked the dirt into neat little furrows, creating a beautiful pattern. I glowed knowing I could do an adult task.

The patio wrapped the front and one side of the house all the way down in a slight pitch to a beautiful meandering ditch. To prevent erosion, Nanita placed lots of stones on the western edge to form a border and planted many shrubs and small trees such as chokecherry and gooseberry, which were native to the area. Mixed in with the scrubs and trees were sunflowers, tall hollyhocks, the many-colored cosmos, and lots of the wild pink Mexican *Rosa de Castilla*. When we sat outside, we enjoyed the fragrance of these special roses.

We loved spending time on the *patio*, but inside my *abuelos'* house was just as entertaining. Leading into the house was an open-air *portal*. This porch was no ordinary *portal*! It took up a whole quarter of the dwelling and was surrounded by gorgeous red and white climbing roses. In the summer, the dining table was set on the *portal* so we could admire the blossoms and enjoy the sweet aroma of the flowers while we ate.

Many evenings after dinner, we happily whirled around the giant *portal* to the music of whatever record Rampo had placed on the Victrola. What fun we had. Both grownups and children swayed and spun until we were out of breath and had to wipe our dripping foreheads. The only person who got a little rest was the one who was cranking the record player.

Oh my, what joy! We could sing at the top of our lungs and no one told us to lower our voices. Occasionally, we would start screaming that a bee was buzzing around in the middle of our antics, but Nanita would swish it away with her apron and we would return to our loud and mostly off-key noisy romps as we tried out new fancy steps.

The *portal* also was used to host informal community dances. It didn't matter if you had a partner. Everyone, young and old, would get up at the same time and dance. The usual group was Mamita, Nanita, Rampo, my sister, my brother, and me. As soon as the neighbors down the valley would hear our beautiful music, they would make their way up the hill to join us. They sometimes came with guitars and violins! Then it became a real dance, and no one ever sat down. If we really were tired, we sat on the porch steps between dances; other than a few chairs there was no furniture on the *portal*, which left plenty of room for dancing.

The *portal* was not built with dancing in mind. Its wooden planks were made of pine and had large knots that would easily fall out with strenuous stomping. When a knot fell out, Rampo stopped the dancing, got the top lid of a can, and used his big hammer and a few nails to fix the hole. Some of the children covered their ears when the loud pounding (certainly not any louder than our music and yelling) of the hammer on the nails commenced. I personally danced to the beautiful staccato sounds. As soon as the nailing was over, we resumed our jumping to the happy polka and *ranchera* music.

Dance parties usually were held in the daytime on Saturdays and Sundays when everyone worked a little less on their *ranchos*. Rampo and Nanita did not have electricity for night time parties. However, they did have a coal oil lantern and would bring it out to the *portal* when it seemed that no one wanted the fun to end. Since the adults worked so hard during the week, they were usually too tired to stay up late.

The *portal* was scrubbed both before and after the party. We had large buckets of hot soapy water that the grownups carted up the steps from where the water had been heated. Using hand rags and a brush, we went, swish, swish, swish. The boards were almost white from so much scrubbing, but they had quite a few splinters, so we had to be extra careful when wiping them dry. I loved the work. My brother was too young to help, and my sister didn't like to do physical work, so I was the only one to help Nanita and Mamita. I earned lots of pats on my head from them for being such a hard worker. I cherished those rewards!

From the *portal*, we entered the house into *la sala*. This living room was a big comfortable room that mostly got used when company came or at night when the family was in the house. The first thing you noticed when entering were the beautiful walls. Rampo and his neighbors had plastered the adobe walls with calcimined white clay, and used a contrasting reddish-brown clay to paint the bottom half of each wall. Even the door openings were framed with the reddish-brown plaster. While Rampo and the neighbors did the rough plastering, the final fine plastering was done by the women in the area, including Nanita. At the top of the walls, next to the ceiling, Nanita stamped flowers using sliced potatoes, lambs-wool, and the same colored plaster.

Crucifixes and pictures of saints hung on the walls. There were also two big-framed pictures of Nanita's grandparents, *Los Abuelitos*. The living room had two windows with beautiful lace curtains that Nanita had made. One window faced the porch and the other faced the apple orchards; both had red geranium plants in coffee cans on the sills.

The wooden floor planks were covered with rag rugs, which, like Mamita's, were made from scraps of material or old clothes. They not only made the floor look pretty, but also provided a nice soft place for walking, especially for us kids that were mostly barefoot. Nanita created all these embellishments with only the items she could find in her home or on the ranch.

Next to the *fogón*, a wood-burning heater stove in one corner of the *sala*, were two traditional high back chairs. One was covered with a red, black, and white Navajo rug that had Nanita's name woven into it. The other chair had a beautifully embroidered cushion made by Nanita. Two wooden rocking chairs with brightly colored hand-made cushions were set next to hand-hewn pine tables that were covered with chintz skirts. On top of the tables, Nanita placed her hand-made white embroidered doilies or long embroidered runners, a couple of family pictures, more pictures of saints, and the ever-present plant potted in a coffee can. The coffee cans, she covered in colorful paper to match the blossoms.

The main attraction of the room was the *altarcito*. This small altar had been a desk, but Nanita made it into a place for her statue of saints, prayer books, and candles. She had a candle lit night and day. That was the gathering place at night for family prayers and for visitors who all knelt before the altar to say prayers. Sometimes they said their prayers aloud and sometimes quietly. Of course, if visitors knelt, Nanita did too and made us follow suit. We were happy they were short prayers and we could quickly run out to play.

However, the huge piece of furniture that caught the eye of most everyone was the Murphy bed. On one wall, there was a large brown-painted wooden plank that sort of looked like a giant closet door, but had some rather large brass and wood handles. I would watch visitors' reactions as they tried not to stare at that wall. Murphy beds were not a common sight in our community. I imagined that maybe they thought it was one of Rampo's unfinished projects. Maybe they thought it was an unfinished part of a wall. Maybe they thought it was the beginning of a closet. Might they wonder why it was painted so nicely? What were they thinking? I never asked.

At night, when our *abuelos* lowered the heavy brown board, it became a huge comfortable bed with a great mattress and many pillows and blankets. I have no idea why they made or bought it, but we never saw one before and we never saw one again. Maybe they were told it would save lots of space in the living room, because it certainly did that. That bed made a nice living-bedroom combination in their small home.

Nanita also had two large travel trunks in *la sala*. Each was painted deep brown. One had a flat top and the other had a round top. Both trunks had strips of tin adorning them with additional pieces of stamped tin and lots of *tachuelas*, large tin tacks. Visitors considered them show pieces. They always commented on their beauty. Nanita loved them because mice could not get in.

The trunks held real treasures. In the trunk with the rounded top, Nanita's stored her prized possessions, including a *mantilla*, some Spanish combs and the traditional black shawl or *tápalo*. She also kept fabric that she would use to make dresses and aprons or a gift for a wedding or baptism. She made everything. There were spools of black and white thread and some spools of white crochet thread. At the very bottom there were some beaded necklaces. There was no expensive jewelry in the house or any kind of silver. In the summer, Nanita would store her jackets and her wool hat to keep them away from the moths. Yes! She also kept mothballs in the trunk, and the toxic smell filled the room whenever she opened the trunk. The trunk with the flat top held winter coats, jackets, hats, vests, extra blankets, and, of course, those hated moth balls.

Regardless of the time of day, when guests or her *comadres* arrived at the front porch, Nanita was ready with the expected invitation to share news, saying, "*¿Cómo están?*" It was a cheerful time with everyone taking time to hug everyone else. If we were lucky and kids had come also, we were told to go out to play, but not to go too far. Junior and I knew we had to stay close to the house, so we could hear Nanita when she called us from the *portal*.

In the meantime, the visitors were escorted into the living room, where all were made comfortable. No one ever visited without sitting a while in the *sala.* That seemed to be a special honor my *abuelos* bestowed on their guests. Seldom did our family go into the living room during the day. We only came in at night to say our prayers in front of the *altarcito.* When the candles were lit, the room became a place of quiet beauty, like a church.

Once the guests entered the living room, Nanita had them sit in her best chairs with the colorful cushions and with little wooden foot benches nearby if needed. The majority of Nanita's friends were short in stature like she was and Nanita thought everyone needed the footstools. When the kids returned from playing, we usually were told to sit on the floor near our parents. As soon as everyone was seated comfortably, Nanita brought in glasses and a pitcher of cool water freshly taken from the deep well close to the house. If she had time, Nanita would flavor the water with herbs.

If guests said they were just passing by and not staying long, Nanita invited them into the kitchen for coffee. As the grownups blew into their blue tin cups to try to cool the coffee enough to drink it, the delicious smell wafted through the air.

Sometimes Nanita added *biscochitos* or *tortillas* with homemade jelly. As she served the food, she sincerely apologized that if had she known they were coming she would have fixed something more appropriate. But the *comadres* always thought Nanita's food was exquisite and typically responded by saying, *"No se preocupe, Comadre. Nomás venimos un ratito para ver como estaba. Hacía tiempo que no la veíamos."* They wanted to reassure her that since they hadn't seen her in some time, they were simply stopping by to see how she was.

Unannounced visits were usually after lunchtime and visitors left before dinner. For guests arriving in the morning, lunch was expected. After a good visit, Nanita would move them from the living room to the *portal* where it was much cooler. She would then go to her kitchen and, while preparing lunch, continue conversing through the screen door that divided the two parts of the house.

At a minimum, Nanita would serve delicious, but soupy, pinto beans with a little red *chile* sauce for flavoring and hand-made flour *tortillas*. If it looked like we were going to run short, you could hear the slap, slap, slap musical sound of Nanita or Mamita making a few extra *tortillas* for the guests. Nanita also served whatever foods she might have prepared earlier for the family.

It was in the kitchen that Mamita, *my abuelos*, and we kids spent most of our time when indoors. The kitchen had a large wood stove. In the middle of the room was a huge wooden table covered with a pretty oilcloth. At either end were two chairs, and on either side were two large *bancos*, benches that Rampo built. Around the room were high cases with shelves for kitchen supplies. Nanita covered the shelves with heavily starched cotton curtains that were held up by two strong nails placed on each side of the mantel. A huge milk can, used as the flour bin, sat in one of the corners. The kitchen included one big window on the west side. It was dressed up with frilly curtains made from flour sacks. The wooden floor, often patched with tin lids to cover the holes when the cursed pine knots fell off, was covered with bright flowered linoleum.

In another corner was an *aguamanil*, a wash basin with a pitcher and a bar of yellow soap purchased from Maloof's Store on Bridge Street in Las Vegas. A mirror was set above the *aguamanil* at eye level for the adults. We never saw ourselves, unless we pushed a chair and stood on it to take a peek.

While we never were allowed to assist with the cooking other than to help wash the dishes or the vegetables, we did come to appreciate the skill Nanita applied to making unforgettable meals. Some foods were only cooked when in season and other foods we had all year long, like *frijoles*.

Summer and spring foods included greens such as *verdolagas* – purslane, or *quelites* – lamb's quarters, a weed similar to dandelions. Nanita and Mamita might sauté these delicate weeds with onions, fresh green *chile*, and scrambled eggs. They might also add the greens to fried pork or beef with tomatoes, onions, garlic, and, of course, fresh green *chile*. We also ate raw cucumbers, radishes, and carrots, or sometimes they would put some of these veggies into soups with potatoes and beef broth.

During the winter, we ate *papas fritas con cebolla y chile colorado* or *chile verde* – fried potatoes with onions and dehydrated red *chile* or green *chile*, *frijoles con chicos o sin chicos* – beans with dehydrated corn kernels or without the corn, or chicken or lamb stew eaten with salty *chaquegue con chile* – a blue corn gruel with *chile*. We also had lots of piping hot stews and soups that contained whichever meats or vegetables were available.

Nanita was famous for her beef gravy made with dried meat. She would have us kids first pound the *carne seca* with smoothed river rocks until we ended up with thin shredded strands of beef and had the gristle separated from the meat. Nanita would then take the product of our hard work and place it in slightly salted boiling water to cook until tender. While waiting, she would make a mouth-watering milk gravy and sautéed onions with other available vegetables.

Once everything was done, Nanita would add the shredded beef and fried vegetables to the gravy. This sauce was ladled over a baked potato or beans and eaten with a hot flour *tortilla*. Yum!

I can't forget the *torta de huevo con chile colorado* – fluffy patties made from egg whites and served with rich red *chile* sauce. We often ate *torta de huevo* during lent. On Christmas, we could count on her making tasty pork *tamales* – corn dough stuffed with shredded pork and red *chile* sauce and steamed.

Everyone in my family had a sweet tooth, so we had lots of desserts and sugary drinks including *pan de anís* – sweet bread flavored with anise, *pan dulce* – small sweet wheat bread, *empanadas* – fruit filled turnovers, and home-made jelly with flour *tortillas*. For drinks, she made hot cocoa, hot sweet tea brewed from herbs grown in the garden or from those found on the ranch property, and *pinole* – roasted ground corn mixed with milk and a combination of sugar or honey, cocoa, cinnamon, vanilla, and other available sweet spices. When the cows were producing milk, we had fresh milk and would squabble over who would drink the thick cream that formed at the top of the milk can. One of my favorite desserts was Nanita's *natillas* – a rich egg and milk custard. Eating at my *abuelos'* house was always a feast.

The final two rooms in the house were the two bedrooms. They did not have doors, but the doorways were covered with flower-designed curtains made by none other than Nanita. In the winter, the curtains were pulled back to allow heat from the *fogón* to seep into the rooms. Nanita and Rampo slept in the biggest room, which had a window that faced the mountains. The small room was reserved for Mamita and Papito, but later it became a storage room, holding everything that was not used on a daily basis.

Each bedroom contained only a double-sized bed. However, these were not ordinary beds. We called them *camaltas* because each was a high bed piled high with *colchones*, hand-made mattresses. When we had lots of company sleeping over, Nanita and Rampo would pull the extra *colchones* off the beds and place them on the floor in the living room, the kitchen, and sometimes even on the porch, when the nights were not too cold. There was always room for whomever needed a place to sleep.

My *abuelos* were wealthy in my eyes. Rampo and Nanita had secured a loan from the federal government to buy their magical high sierra arid *ranchito* and worked diligently night and day to get the land to produce. It required lot of hard work because their farm equipment was limited to an old rusty and weather-beaten plow, a huge scoop, and a large rake pulled by a team of horses. Everything else was done by hand or by the equipment that was borrowed from a neighbor. For payment of the use of the neighbors' machinery, my *abuelos* helped them with their farming tasks, such as plowing, raking, winnowing various grains, and other general chores.

Most of my *abuelos'* neighbors were not formally educated, but all were very honest and extremely hard-working individuals. A handshake was all the legality that was needed to transact business. These cash poor farmers were self-employed, and only during early autumn when they migrated to the harvest fields in Colorado did they have a little money. They immediately used this money to pay their year-long debts at the local grocery store as well as to buy the family provisions for the upcoming winter.

Rampo was one of the few land owners that had a job away from home that provided a little spare cash year-round, but he typically used that money to help support other families in the valley. My *abuelos* never let anyone go hungry, knowing that the people in their community were suffering from a lack of work due to the Great Depression. When my Rampo would see a family coming up their dirt path, he'd call Nanita by her name and say, "*Juanita, agrégales más agua a los fríjoles y has las tortillas más chiquititas. Viene visita.*" By adding more water to the beans and making the *tortillas* smaller, Nanita was then ready for company.

It was unbelievable that my *abuelos'* money went so far and for so many good causes. Whatever little money they had left after shopping, Nanita would put it in an empty jelly glass jar, like a piggy bank. She kept the jar hidden in the flour bin, which was a big, slightly dented tin milk container with a rather narrow opening at the top. Digging for the jar in the flour was not all that easy, but it sure was a safe hiding place and as secure as a bank. Nanita would say to no one in particular, "*Aquí no hay ladrones, pero es mejor no tentar.*" She was right not to tempt fate even though there were no thieves in the neighborhood! Nanita was not only talented, she was also a wise and practical woman. She and Rampo made a welcoming home filled with good food and good company.

Little wonder I called this my "happy place."

Chapter 4: Special Treats

Nanita found lots of ways to surprise us, but the most pleasing were her treats.

Sometimes she would unexpectedly bring us a snack in the middle of the morning, sometimes in the middle of the afternoon, or maybe even just before going to bed. We never knew when we would have one of her special food delights. Her reason for the treats was because we were good, as she would explain simply, *"Porque fueron buenos."* For us hungry kids, it was the perfect reward.

Occasionally Nanita would bring in fresh picked lettuce leaves and then wash them in a pan full of icy, cold water from the well. After briefly soaking the lettuce, she would shake them and wrap the leaves in a cotton towel for a minute or two. Then she would call us and when we arrived, she would sprinkle the leaves with a dash of vinegar and some sugar. Sweet and sour treats were at the top of our snack list!

Esquite was another treat we often had because Rampo grew corn in his fields and we had plenty to shuck and eat in various ways. Nanita would sprinkle sugar over the damp kernels of corn and toast them in the oven until they turned a crunchy rich brown caramelized color. It was our version of Kettle Corn.

We sometimes had *buñuelos* or *sopaipillas*. These light as air-fried wheat dough pastries were introduced by the early Spaniards and still are enjoyed here in New Mexico. The dough for the *buñuelos* was rolled thin, cut into squares with a knife and fried in hot oil. The *buñuelos* came out crispy and thin, like the Mexican version of the elephant ears sold in booths at fairs. We ate these golden-brown delicacies by sprinkling them with sugar and cinnamon. For the *sopaipillas*, the dough was rolled less thin and cut using the lids of jars to form round shapes. Once fried and puffy, we poured honey into the cavity and let each bite melt in our mouths.

Some nights we had *piñones,* which were picked from our *piñon* pine trees behind the house. When in season, these delicate little seeds were roasted in a skillet on top of the stove with a sprinkle of salt. If it was a large batch, they were put in the oven. Nanita or Mamita often sampled the hot *piñones* until they felt they had the right dark-brown color and the seeds had a creamy, nutty flavor. Once the nuts were roasted to perfection, Nanita would place them in a bowl on the kitchen table. We were quick to grab handfuls, shell them, and eat the warm mouthwatering seeds. We made sure to make neat little piles of the shells as we cracked the nut with our teeth just like we were trained. One of us always wiped the shells off the table when we were done eating. Nanita would be so pleased!

I also loved my Nanita's *galletitas*. These cookies were made with only three ingredients: flour, butter, and sweetened condensed milk. I could also not forget her *bolillos de anís,* and the crunchy sound we made when biting into the *anís.* We did not get these bread rolls often because they were served only during special holiday meals. I loved them hot, fresh out of the oven, but our grownups thought we should never eat hot bread because it would hurt our stomachs and produce *empacho.*

Even though we all had to work hard every day at the *ranchito,* I never felt so special as the time Nanita baked me a chocolate birthday cake for my eleventh birthday.

Nanita stopped her daily chores in the middle of the afternoon, put sticks of dry wood into the stove and let them burn until they became hot coals. I then watched her closely as she mixed the ingredients for my special cake. She combined flour with a little sugar, added some shortening, a big pinch of baking powder, and two fresh brown eggs from the chicken coop. To moisten the mixture, she slowly poured in milk. I don't know how she did it, but Nanita never followed recipes.

She next checked to see if the oven was hot enough by sprinkling a few drops of cold water inside the cooker and watched carefully as the water bounced and made a hissing sound; that was when she knew the oven was hot enough to bake my cake. She then poured the batter into two round cake tins and slid them into the hot oven.

While the cake was baking, she made the icing. Of course, we had no powdered sugar. Come to think of it, I never even knew such a thing existed until I took a home economics class in high school, but who needed it? Nanita took some regular white sugar and added dry cocoa powder. When the mixture blended into a beautiful dark brown texture, she added a few drops of milk and water for it to be slightly runny.

Once the cake finished baking, she cooled it for a few minutes on the windowsill. Nanita then bathed it in that brown silky icing. We had no candles for the cake, but she stepped out onto the porch and plucked a beautiful pink rose from the trellis and stuck it into the middle of the cake.

This birthday clinched it – I knew I was Nanita's favorite. She must have loved that I entertained her with my insatiable zest for life and prayed with her any time of the day. Little wonder I thrived under Nanita's special attention and of course her many hugs and kisses.

Community

Chapter 5: Leave Nothing to Chance

Religion in our family was as much a daily activity as breathing.

And preparing for Sunday church was as much a ritual as washing up before supper. However, preparations took longer and started on Saturdays.

The first chore was to wash Rampo's Model A Ford. The car, while not new, was carefully maintained. After every trip on the dusty road and especially before Sunday, Rampo drove the car to Las Manuelitas Creek to get washed.

The narrow creek had a rocky bottom and we could dip our buckets into the water without mixing it with sand. Rampo, while sitting with Nanita on the bank, would wave his hand in the direction of the hood and tell us to get the car nice and wet. He did not want the paint scratched, so he would instruct us not to wipe it down until we rinsed off all the dust first.

"*Bueno*, Rampo," I would say as I pretended to aim for the car, but in truth I was aiming at Junior. He was used to my tricks and watched me carefully out of the corner of his eye. One time, Junior seemed to be bending over to fill his bucket with water as I gingerly walked over toward him trying not to slip on the rocks in the creek. Without warning I swung my bucket to splash him with my water. As I launched my bucket of water in the air, he quickly straightened up, and launched his filled bucket at me. There was a great clash of water in the air. The water from our buckets collided and rained over both of us. We were drenched. We would call endings like this a tie. Neither beat the other one in the wet contest.

We loved when Rampo would join us. He would roll up his pant legs and we could see his hairy bare feet. They looked like white fish in the shallow, clear water.

We weren't brave enough to actually throw an entire bucket of water at Rampo, so we would pretend to aim our buckets at the part of the car closest to Rampo and splash him accidently in the process. "Oops, Rampo." Sorry, I would apologize meekly, but not so innocently.

Always good natured, Nanita would remind us to not wet Rampo because he had to drive the car back to the house. "*Bueno*, Nanita," I responded, already plotting my next move. It was not fair, but we loved it when Rampo would reciprocate by pouring a bucket of water over each of our heads. We would laugh and laugh and then the water game was on again.

The car was finally rinsed after mostly wetting each other and it was time to get serious and wipe it down with old rags. These were not just any old rags, like the faded old towel we typically used. No, these were Rampo's old torn and tattered long-johns and leftover pieces of Nanita's worn dresses that she could not turn into an apron or quilt. We did not have to worry about making sure the car glowed, the wax had been rubbed off long ago. We just needed to use the old rags to dry off the excess water so that Rampo could drive it back up the hill to the house.

After dinner, we would rest on the *portal*, waiting for Nanita to announce, *"Antes de la puesta del sol, tenemos una cosa más que hacer."* She really didn't have to tell us that before sunset, we had one more thing to do. We knew like clockwork, just before nightfall the next cleansing ritual would begin. It now was our turn, and we knew the routine well. Nanita would tell us to cleanse the body in preparation for cleansing the soul, saying, *"Limpia el cuerpo en preparación para limpiar el alma."*

However, taking a bath was not as easy as washing the car. Our *abuelos* did not have running water and did not own a bathtub. That's right! At the *rancho* you had to go in search of water. We had to use Nanita's buckets to scoop water from the nearby ditch when it ran clear. If the ditch water ran too low or muddy, we had to walk through the orchards, cross a marsh, and get water from their well. Sometimes we even had to walk further down to Las Manuelitas Creek when the well was dry. This weekly quest was my first lesson about the importance of water conservation. Every drop counted, even to take a simple bath!

While we lugged the buckets full of water into the house, Nanita (and Mamita when she was with us) would heat up the stove with Rampo's chopped wood. They would then take our buckets and pour the water into the stove's attached *calentón*, a chamber for heating the water. Next a large tin tub was pushed behind the stove, which provided enough space to bathe. Nanita hung old sheets around the tub for privacy and to keep the corner warm while we bathed.

Before the bathing ceremony commenced, Nanita and Mamita would pour a couple of buckets of hot water from the *calentón* into the tub and then add cold water to make the bathwater luxuriously warm. I remember vividly that next to the tub was a wooden bench where Nanita would place a bar of her hand-made yellow soap, a towel, a washcloth, a bottle of vinegar with a tablespoon, and a large tin bucket of cold water with a big cobalt blue enameled dipper.

Oh! There was the usual scramble about which one of us was going to be first. Vera would pout, "*Yo debo ser primero. ¡Yo soy la mayor!*" Then Junior would shout, "*No. Yo debo de ser el primero. ¡Yo soy el menor!*"

As the middle child, I usually kept quiet because I knew my sister and brother would not be the ones to decide. Mamita or Nanita would announce who was to go first. The rest of us had to wait patiently for our turn.

Once it was our turn, we washed our bodies and hair with the homemade yellow bar of soap. Since water was scarce, we all had to bathe in the same water. Being last was no fun because Mamita or Nanita would add heated water to the tub in which the others had bathed. That was why we all wanted to be first. But there was one major advantage to being last. The last bather could stay longer to play in the tub now filled to the top with warm water.

A portion of the hot water was always saved to rinse our hair when we were through bathing. Nanita would mix a little vinegar and cold water from the dipper to the warm water for this ritual. On occasion, Nanita would make *amole* by crushing the yucca root and turning it into a foamy shampoo. The *amole* made my black hair shinny and soft without the vinegar smell.

Because I had such long thick hair, Mamita or Nanita usually washed my hair in a washbasin set on the *aguamanil* before I bathed. My hair required a longer time to dry and Nanita and Mamita believed that going to bed with wet hair would make you sick.

When Nanita washed my hair she would exclaim over its beauty, "*¡Va, que cabello tan lindo!*" But I hated my long, heavy hair, and I secretly wished it was cut short like my girlfriends' hair.

After bathing, we had to be careful when drying ourselves so as not to hit the hot stove with our elbows. Getting ready for bed was easy, since we did not have much of a wardrobe. We girls slept in our panties and full slips. My brother slept in his underwear in the summer or long johns in the winter. Since it was believed that we would catch a cold going barefoot after a bath we had to put on our only pair of shoes for the rest of the evening.

Our chores were not yet over. Before the bath water was thrown out, we had to scrub our socks in the tub. We rinsed our socks almost nightly, but on Saturday night they got a good washing in the sudsy tub. We would then hang them to dry overnight on a wire that had been stretched high in the bathing area behind the stove. In the morning the socks would be toasty warm.

The next chore was to have Nanita and Mamita help us clip our fingernails and toenails. Nanita only had a pair of dull scissors so our nails always look jagged. I would think to myself when they were being cut that they were also way too short.

After the nails, came the ear exam. Both ears were inspected for dirt and wax. Nothing got passed over by Nanita and Mamita. Every part of our bodies had to be clean. To be honest, I looked forward to our Saturday baths. This was the only warm bath we would take for the week. In our home in Las Vegas, we could only afford to take cold baths or take what we called a "sponge bath." Mamita would warm just enough water on the stove and put it in a dishpan for us to wash ourselves. We would start from the top of our heads and end with wiping the bottom of our feet since they were the dirtiest part of our bodies. Always before we sponged ourselves, Mamita would tap the top of our heads with cold water. In accordance with this old tradition, she believed that if your feet got wet, you had to immediately wet your head to keep from getting sick.

The only cleaning detail both our parents and *abuelos* overlooked was our tooth care. Following an old family tradition, we would stick a damp forefinger into the box of baking soda and rub our teeth. We never used toothbrushes because we could not afford to buy them. In fact, it was not until I was in the third grade when the teachers passed out free toothbrushes that I first saw one. Because our toothbrushes were so precious, we left them at home, so when we visited Nanita and Rampo, we reverted to the nightly rubbing of our teeth with baking soda. It did a good job of shining our teeth, but it never brushed out the plaque. As a result, two of us suffered great tooth decay at an early age.

I recall crying and telling Mamita that my tooth hurt, asking her to feel the big bump on my gum. The bump was a pustule of pus and it was ever so painful. The cure was a little baking soda applied with the finger on the sore spot. Sometimes she ground up an aspirin and applied the powder to the gum. The pain remained; only sleep relieved it for a while.

When we were all done, Rampo and Nanita would go to the living room and pull down the big Murphy bed from the wall. This bed is where all three of us slept. I came to believe that the Murphy bed was built special just for us kids.

Before hopping into bed, we all knelt in front of Nanita's *altarcito* for the evening prayer. We were always happy that the prayers were short, so we could have our snack before we went to bed. It was usually *esquite*, toasted corn kernels covered with a little caramelized sugar; there went the dental care!

Nothing was left to chance: we were clean and well prepared for Sunday church, or so we thought. Nanita would remind us of one final task while tucking us into bed. We were to examine our consciences by reviewing the Ten Commandments of God before we went to sleep. Did I steal? Did I honor my mother and father? Did I cuss? Did I lie? Nanita wanted us to think carefully about what we might have failed to do so that we would know what to confess to the priest before the mass started on Sunday.

I just wanted to sleep!

CHAPTER 6: ONWARD TO CHURCH

Traveling to church was another test of our faith.

La Virgen de Guadalupe Church was only two and a half miles from my *abuelos' ranchito*. But sometimes it took as much effort to get there on Sunday mornings as it did to get ready on Saturday nights.

When Rampo's Model A Ford was not working, which happened often, or the dirt roads were impassable due to rain or heavy snow, we would ride to church in an old-fashioned covered wagon. It looked just like the ones the pioneers used to cross the plains of the west, only a little bit smaller.

For the trip, my *abuelos* prepared the wagon box with a big old wool mattress, ancient pillows, and heavily used multicolored homemade quilts. It looked like a lively gypsy wagon and made the bumpy, usually dusty ride, a little more bearable. In the summer, the blankets were simply used for sitting. In the winter, they came in handy to cover us from the bitter cold. We would snuggle into the pillows and blankets, with Nanita fussing over us to stay still so we could get toasty warm. And, of course, if we got thirsty during the trip, there was the ever-present Mason jar filled with clear fresh creek water. If we were extra good, Nanita would give us a store-bought ginger snap cookie or two instead of the usual *biscochitos*.

The team of heavy plodding horses that did the hard work on our farm was used to pull our wagon. They were gentle male horses, with the odd names of Dick and June. Where did my *abuelos*, who spoke little English, come up with those names? I wondered if it was because all three of us grandchildren were born in June, or if the names reminded them of our second-grade school books with the Dick and Jane characters. Maybe June sounded more masculine than Jane. I never did ask my *abuelos* how they came up with the names of the horses. Rampo never used a whip to prod the horses, so my brother and I would yell at them to speed up until Nanita shushed us.

If it looked as if it might rain or snow, Grandpa and Nanita would say, *"Entoldar el carro."* Covering the wagon cart meant mounting large high bows in the front, back, and middle of the wagon cart, and then covering the bows with a huge white canvas. To make it fit taut, they would tie the canvas down in several places.

When finished, Rampo would announce that we were ready for any kind of weather. It was fun riding in a real covered wagon. But there was a problem. We could only look out through the front or back openings, so my siblings and I pushed and shoved for the best views.

Once on the road, Nanita would start singing *cánticos*. We all sang along the best we could. Her voice was high-pitched and rather shrill, but she knew all the words to the hymns, and she loved to sing. We often sang the following *cántico* on our way to church:

O, María, Madre mía
O, consuelo del mortal
Ampararme y guiarme
A la patria celestial.

Oh, Mary, our dear mother
Oh, comfort of all mortals
Protect us and guide us
to our heavenly homeland.

As we traveled on, I imagined we looked just like the covered wagons in the western movies. I was proud of myself thinking just like Vera and her movie star magazines! The image disappeared when we met our *abuelos'* friends along the road. Out of respect for our elders, we children had to be quiet and extra polite. We were to be seen and not heard.

Some of the parishioners who lived on the other side of the mountain along a green valley seemed to be a little better off than our *abuelos* and us. One family composed of parents and several beautifully dressed children rode to church in a black surrey led by skinny prancing black trotters. The gentleman driving the horses always tipped his hat at our family as they passed our less agile horses. I often wondered if their ride was as bumpy as ours. The children certainly looked more comfortable. They even had a black-fringed top to keep the sun off of them. And they had two rows of padded seats to ride on. The seats were high off the floor of the surrey. It seemed like pure luxury to me. I never figured out a way to ask them what it felt like as they weren't particularly friendly.

After about an hour on the road, we could finally see *La Virgen de Guadalupe* Church in Sapelló. The church was considered a big one as far as village churches went. It was an adobe structure painted white with a shiny tin roof, bright blue window frames, and a double-door entryway. It stood in the middle of a big open meadow with the home of our priest to the left and slightly behind the church. What made it unique was its location right in the middle of a beautiful grassy meadow not far from the Sapelló River. In the summer, you could see all kinds of pretty wildflowers surrounding the church when it was not too dry.

A very rocky and narrow road came up to the two old wooden doors that never closed quite right. It seemed they were made with permanent sag. There were also large wooden planks in front of the doors for us to scrape off the mud clinging to our shoes, especially in the wet season.

When we arrived, we joined the semi-circle at the front of the church. No one ever parked on the actual road leading to the church. The automobiles parked on one side of the semi-circle and the rest of us parked our wagons on the other side. Those who rode on horseback tied their horses to the fence that surrounded the church property.

The village neighbors soon greeted Nanita, Rampo, and Mamita. They shook hands and received warm hugs from everyone that arrived. As my brother and I jumped off the wagon, we must have looked like we just got out of bed. With lots of tsk tsks, Nanita and Mamita would grab us and hold us still until they straightened out our clothes to make us look presentable. There always seemed to be a breeze in the meadow and it did funny things to my long screw curls, which would spring every which way except down where they belonged. My brother's cowlick got put in its place with a pat and a little saliva from Mamita. My older sister Vera did her own grooming and tried hard to look grownup before walking to the church.

We strolled the short distance to the church entrance through tall weedy flowers and more than a few noisy bees. We stopped at the wooden platform in front of the church door to shake the dust from our shoes. When it rained, we scraped away the rusty brown mud from our shoes. If the ground was too muddy, we would put on an older pair of shoes and carry a better pair in our hands to change into once we reached the church. The muddy shoes obviously stayed outside.

Entering the church always surprised me. It was filled with light as it had large, high, and clear windows on both sides of the church walls. The bright sunbeams were right at home in God's house. At the front of the church was an altar that was surrounded by a white picket fence. Between the windows were many saints painted with bright colors on the plastered walls. The beautiful hand-carved *santos* had long ago disappeared from the church. In the 1800s, the newly arrived anglos offered to buy the *santos*. The community, not realizing their value, sold.

Upon entering the church, we always placed a hand in the holy water bowl next to the entrance and made the sign of the cross. I am sure we looked respectable and pious enough for Sunday confession and mass. Having surmounted the challenge of getting to church, my next challenge was to figure out what I was going to confess to the priest before mass.

Chapter 7: Memorable Blessings

God in his wisdom created church for more than praying.

It was where we went to rest, to forget for a little while about our poverty, and to connect with our neighbors. Everyone would leave their isolated *ranchos* to learn the latest news, enjoy each other's company, and tell fun stories or jokes. Each Sunday, I looked forward to discovering which purpose or blessing would suit me best.

Confession was always offered before mass, so once we walked into church, I had to focus my attention on deciding what to confess. At my age I didn't commit grave sins. My sins typically consisted of squabbling with a sibling or having had "bad" thoughts. These thoughts were usually limited to something serious like wanting to use the word "damn" after having stubbed a toe. Of course, we would never actually say the word, but just thinking about it was considered sinful. I would scare Junior by whispering to him, "Nanita says, *Si decimos esa palabra, nos vamos a ir al infierno.*" Threatening him with Nanita's warning about going to hell if we used bad words was all it took to keep him quiet.

Waiting silently in line to have the priest hear our confessions, I was grateful to have some time to rethink my sins. Sometimes I would pile up more sins while waiting. Looking around, playing, or poking someone in the ribs could easily count as a sin; at least that is what Nanita would tell us when asking us to stand still in the line for confession.

Before long, it was my turn to go into the confessional. I opened the curtain and knelt on a bench in the dark cubicle. As my eyes adjusted, I could see the outline of the priest's head through a little window covered with lattice woodwork in front of me. I dutifully began, Bless me Father, for I have sinned....

My penance nearly always was to recite two Hail Marys. During the following week, the kids in our community compared the prayers we needed to pray in order to have our sins forgiven. With that information, we easily decided who was the biggest sinner, and who might even go to hell. We never found out if the adults played this penance game. I asked, but never got an answer. "*No se,*" was the response to my question.

Once confession was over, we went to find a seat for the upcoming mass. There were several rows of creaky, wooden pews in the front half of the church. It was easy to make them screech by varying our movements, but my brother and I were pinched and admonished to sit still and concentrate on God. We whispered that the pews were making noise by themselves, but no one ever believed us.

Estarse quieto was a sign of growing up, but we were just children and couldn't make ourselves be quiet or still. Besides, the kneeling benches had no padding, and we tried to avoid them by sitting or standing as much as possible. During certain parts of the mass, we were made to kneel without moving. The grownups seemed to take it well, but we were miserable and hoped for the part where we could stand up and wiggle.

Other than the altar and the few pews at the front, the rest of the church was empty. The men usually stood at the back. I'm not sure why, but maybe it had to do with ancient church traditions when men and women sat separately so they would pay better attention during worship.

An enjoyable part of mass for me was the music. The stairs leading to the choir loft were on the right side of the entrance to the church. It housed a small organ that apparently no one knew how to play. Occasionally someone banged out a tune, but for the most part the organ remained covered with a gray, linen cloth. Although no one seemed to know where the organ had come from, all the parishioners were proud of it.

The choir was composed of all the teenage girls who attended mass, whether they could sing or not. The age, not the voice, was the criterion. My sister, who could not sing herself out of a paper bag, had to leave the family and trudge up the stairs.

But who cared about the choir and the organ when we had such lovely church bells that rang three times before mass? We could hear the clear melodic peals all over the near mountains and valleys. It was a beautiful sound that called us to church, and the bell let us know if we had to hurry or if we could go leisurely. The bells served as a giant timepiece. Few people owned watches, and one small clock per household was the standard. Rampo had a vest watch tied to a chain, and many a neighbor asked him the time.

And, oh! the hats! All women, young and old, covered their heads in reverence to our Lord. Some owned stylish hats; others wore large black or white lace *mantillas* or multicolored cotton bandanas or scarfs; and some wore only a small piece of lace held down in place with a bobby pin. A few older women covered their heads with black *tápalos*. One neighbor, Doña Julianita always wore one, and the black shawl made her look old and tired even though she was only in her early fifties. Maybe she was tired, but the *tápalo* only emphasized her age.

In contrast to the women, the men and boys removed their hats or caps when approaching the church. During mass, they placed their hats on the floor or on the windowsills. A few would hold them throughout the services and sometimes nervously twirled the hats in their hands. They did not put them back on their heads until they were outside the church. It did not matter if the weather was hot, raining, or snowing; it did not matter if you were bald: all men obeyed the church hat rule.

During the summer, girls who were too young to sing in the choir and who owned a white dress were encouraged to wear them to church. The church seemed brighter with the perennial white of the first Holy Communion dresses. I was proud to wear my white outfit, even though it was used and Mamita had to alter it to fit me.

I remember one priest in particular, a handsome Dutchman who spoke heavily accented English and even worse Spanish. He knew absolutely nothing about the northern New Mexico Spanish culture. But oh! We loved how hard he worked to nurture our spirits in whatever way he could. Many a time on our way home, we could not remember his sermon, but we always remembered the mistakes he made in Spanish. They were so funny. Sometimes the priest used words that had double meaning for us. As we giggled and commented on his errors, Nanita would desperately try to get the conversation back to the sermon. Even at the risk of making her angry, we would break into fits of laughter. Rampo, sitting on the board that served as a seat on the wagon, pretended not to hear the commotion, but I'm sure he enjoyed the hilarity and the ruckus. His sense of humor was much broader than Nanita's.

One Sunday stands out in my mind. The priest had told us the church needed some serious repair and we needed to raise money for the work. In the sermon, he motivated everyone to double up on our *fiestas*. As a little girl who loved celebrations, I certainly agreed with this plan. It would mean twice as much fun.

The priest was so pleased about this new venture that in his excitement he garbled his Spanish and said that we would use the first amount of money collected for the *fundillo* of the church. We did not laugh loudly in the church, but the murmur was more than audible. He had used *fundillo*, which translated as 'bottom' or 'bum'. He meant to say the *fundación* or foundation of the church. That was the Sunday Nanita and Rampo laughed all the way home. They repeated this story often when recalling the Spanish of our earnest priest.

This earnest priest relied on the community to maintain the church. My *abuelos* and their *compadres, comadres,* and *vecinos* were very involved in this effort and took turns each year to lead the church projects as *mayordomos*. They took care of everything and made sure that the church was especially clean. We often helped them, usually on a Saturday, which meant another long trip from the house to the church.

The *mayordomos* were great motivators, and they got the neighbors to help with the heavy chores such as plastering walls with mud or helping with the yearly painting. There was also a person, called the *sacristán*, who physically helped the priest. He assisted the priest with putting on his vestments, and he made sure the altar was completely ready for the mass. He lit the candles and performed all the other necessary preparations.

By being selected *mayordomos*, my *abuelos* were the sponsors of the major church *fiestas* that were held once a year. As a result, the *mayordomos,* their families, and helpers became very popular members of the church. Everyone I knew in Las Manuelitas and Sapelló was poor, but we never lacked the opportunity to help others or to have a *fiesta*.

Chapter 8: Las Fiestas

A simple *fiesta* brought great joy.

My *abuelos* just needed a musician or two, and they were not hard to find. Many of the locals played at least one instrument and they never charged for their services.

Once the musicians volunteered their talent, a *fiesta* date was set. The *fiesta* could take place at a home, on the church grounds, in the Sapelló dance hall, in the school house, or under a grove of trees; it could be anywhere in the community. In no time, *entablados* would be used to make a platform of wooden planks for dancing. Children, teens, singles, parents, and the elderly danced together and alone. With the addition of potluck dishes made by all the neighbors and *compadres*, we could eat, dance, and have a great time all afternoon.

During the summer, there were saints' days to celebrate, including those of Santa Ana, San Juan, and San Lorenzo. The church sponsored *fiestas*, but there were also *fiestas* for baptisms, birthdays, anniversaries, weddings, and for no particular reason. A *fiesta* was on because we wanted one.

For me, the best part of the church *fiestas* were *los vendibles.* Typically, these food stands were set-up close to the church under the many cottonwoods growing along the Sapelló River. In the peak of summer, there were lots of wild flowers and beautiful green grasses. Sometimes we had to step on the grasses and flowers to get near the stands; the plants were like fragrant green sidewalks.

Knowing when the *fiestas* would be held, our *abuelos* would save their pennies and nickels for us to buy food. *Fiestas* served hot steaming beans with red and green *chile, posole, chicos*, beef stews, and sometimes ribs. For dessert, you would find *sopaipillas, biscochitos, empanadas, pasteles,* bread pudding, and even *natillas*. For drinks, they served Kool-Aid and hot coffee. While it was the same food we had at home, it was fun to buy it from someone else. We especially liked buying from our *comadres* because they gave us extra-large servings. If we ran out of money, they sometimes gave us food or drink for free.

It was always the women who worked the shifts in the stands. They would dress up in their best clothes and wear beautiful bright aprons. When their time was up, they gathered in groups of *comadres* and caught up with the community news. It was the only time they had to socialize. The *comadres* had happy faces and you could hear their laughter all day long. They only were interrupted if one of their children needed attention.

People—young and old—danced before, while, and after eating. There was an occasional break for the musicians, but if someone else knew how to play, the dancing continued.

Horse-racing was a big affair because we all had horses. The young men liked to show off their skills to their girlfriends. The older people sat around and admired the horsemanship and the horses themselves. The majority of the horses were small and skinny. Oh! Rampo had the only two big horses in the whole community, but they never were used for racing; they were too slow.

All afternoon, the young men with horses would compete in a game called *El Gallo*. The Rooster definitely was not a horse race. A poor rooster would be wrapped in a cloth and buried in extra soft dirt in the middle of the race lane with its neck and head well above ground. The young men would then lengthen their stirrups in anticipation of the dare devil riding that was to come. They would ride at break neck speed, lower themselves to one side of the horse and try to pull the rooster out of the dirt by the head with one hand. I saw a few riders miss the *gallo* and slide out of their saddles. Falling in front of their girlfriends made the young men very embarrassed. Luckily, I never saw anyone get hurt. A few did manage to snatch the rooster and it became their prize.

I only saw the game of *El Gallo* played with a live rooster one summer. During the other summers that I was with my *abuelos*, the race organizers buried bottles of wine with the top exposed, so that the competitors could pull them out. I wondered if the bottle was easier to grab or if somebody felt sorry for the rooster. I decided that everybody had roosters, but few had money to buy wine, and that is probably why they replaced the prize. Funny enough, the name of the race never changed; it was always *El Gallo*.

The games for the children consisted mostly of running and chasing each other. Sometimes we fell, and our mothers admonished us not to play so rough. But as soon as the hurt was gone, we were off running and yelling again. We also jumped lots of rope during those afternoons. Someone always had a rope in his or her wagon. They were usually thick, heavy and hard to turn, but that did not stop us from our game.

When the *fiesta* was held near the river, both boys and girls spent lots of time throwing rocks into the water. The aim was always to see who threw the farthest. There was loud cheering for the person who was the lucky winner. We also spent time searching for flat stones to skip across the water. The winner was the one who could bounce the rock the furthest on the surface of the water. While I was absolutely no good at that game, Junior often was the champ. When we got tired of rock throwing, we took off our shoes and stood in the water while continuing to yell at each other. We were a noisy bunch. Even though there was never enough water in which to actually swim, we had fun. Toward the end of the afternoon, everyone knew the fiesta was over. The priest blessed all of us and thanked us for our donations. It was now time to pack up and take all our belongings back to the cars or wagons. Every adult and child helped. Before sunset, we headed home as the last rays of sunshine shone like a beacon to guide us.

On a few occasions, we would see men drinking from a *flate.* Each would take a swig from the transparent brown flask and pass it around to the other men; I never saw a woman take a drink.

After the *fiesta*, Nanita would sometimes complain that she had seen so-and-so with some *mula*, and that sharing moonshine was why some of the men had gotten tipsy. She would repeat, *"Nunca falta un borracho tonto."* Even though she complained that there's always a dumb drunk who has to ruin a party, I saw it differently. Despite the interruption from the *borrachos,* I couldn't help but recollect the great time I had at the *fiesta* and look forward to the next gathering.

I loved my *abuelos'* community. The people knew how to have fun and how to be pious at the same time.

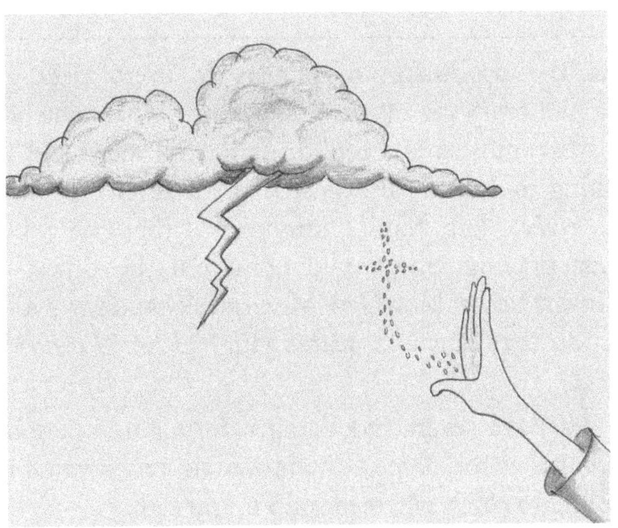

Chapter 9: Nanita's Miracles

When water was scarce, the community could count on Nanita for one of her many miracles.

Nanita encouraged all the women and children, and sometimes some of the men, to form lines to pray in the parched fields to seek divine intervention for rain. No one questioned her orders. They all brought their statues to the first field. Those that had a few wild flower blossoms in their gardens cut or deadheaded the flower heads and brought them in their buckets.

As we walked from field to field, we children spread the flowers while we all sang *cánticos* at the top of our lungs. Then we prayed loudly to the saints to ask God to find it in His mercy to send us rain. Usually we prayed to San Isidro, patron saint of farmers, and to San Lorenzo, patron saint of the poor. Our march through the dusty fields in the blistering sun would last two to three hours. Everyone was wet with perspiration and colored by the dust that stuck to our faces. We were a sight and hoped that God would take pity on us.

After the procession of prayers to every field ended, Nanita had everyone return to her house where she became the hostess and served a cool drink of well water and a little something to eat. She always shared whatever food she had. As the *vecinos* left, Nanita admonished these neighbors to continue praying. She would point out the tiniest white cloud in the bright blue New Mexican sky and say with deep conviction that rain was near, saying, "*¡Mira! La lluvia casi está aquí.*"

We did have several good rains during this period. The *ranchito* was at the base of the mountain and located in the right place to catch whatever rain might fall.

We sometimes experienced short, but severe weather storms with lots of loud clapping and rolling thunder along with bright, sometimes eerie, lightning. Such a storm often brought large-sized hail, which destroyed the crops that were stressed from the lack of steady rain.

One afternoon, we heard a roaring thunderclap very close by and saw the heavens open up with lightning streaks. Nanita got into her mode of praying and quickly told us to pull out our rosaries. "*Saquen el rosario,*" she said.

Nanita believed our rosaries would protect us from all the impending evil the clouds would bring. Praying loudly, she quickly went to the kitchen and took out a box of salt. Picking up her pace, she ran to the edge of the porch and started throwing fistfuls of salt into the sky in the form of a large cross. At the same time she loudly prayed, "*Santo niño ayúdanos. Que no nos vaya ser mal tanta lluvia. Necesitamos lluvia, pero no tanta. Ayúdanos Tatita Dios – Ayúdanos.*" She wanted help from little Jesus, but she also knew not to ask for too much rain.

All the while, the rest of us repeated her prayer loudly for rain. When she finished with her salty sign making, we knelt on the porch floor and prayed the *rosario* again. We began with, *"Padre nuestro que estás en el cielo."* Right as we called on our father who is in heaven, the rain started falling. We got wet as the rain swept into the porch, but nobody moved or complained. We knew that through the intervention of Nanita, our prayers were heard.

As soon as the last mystery of the rosary was prayed, Nanita instructed us children to run with her to the little tool shed. It was now pouring, and we were sopping wet. Nanita told us to take the hoes, rakes, and shovels to the patio and lay them in the form of crosses before running back onto the porch. No lightning struck us! Nanita's angels were *siempre* looking out for us.

On other days, when the rain came down in sheets, Nanita would have us run into the house and fetch the saints from her *altarcito.* We put the statues on the windowsills, so they would calm the storm and bring us only the right amount of water. Of course, we had to say the rosary to make sure our prayers would be answered.

Once, after an extremely loud clap of thunder, the house shook and we could see that up the ravine a tree and bushes were now on fire. Despite the thunder, it did not look like rain was eminent. Our *abuelos* organized us into a small fire brigade armed with pails of water, shovels, and lots of wet *guangoches.* Rampo said the water-soaked gunny sacks would be the best equipment we had. Off we ran around and over boulders until we reached the fire. We found a tree had been split into two; both pieces were burning and igniting the dry pine needles around them.

We worked hard, mostly moving rocks, so we could get shovels full of dirt to put on the fire. By the time we were finished, all of us were a sooty mess. We had smudged faces and dirty, wild looking hair. Before descending the mountainside,

Nanita had us kneel under a majestic ponderosa and pray thanks for seeing the fire in time to keep it from spreading. We also thanked the patron saint of families, "*¡Gracias, San José!*"

Prayers, faith, and love for the land made my *abuelos* strong. I knew they could overcome anything. I prayed that I would be as strong as *mis abuelos* when I grew up.

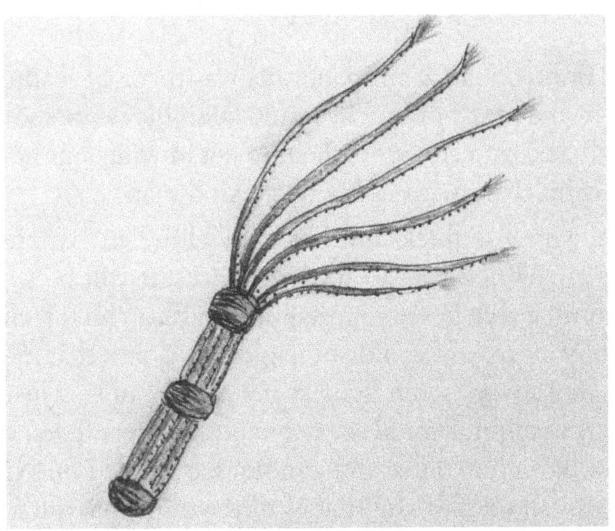

Chapter 10: My First Penitente Encounter

"Just wait until you hear the moans," said Tita, my friend who lived across the creek from the *ranchito*.

We were looking at the *chicotes* hanging on a wall in her parents' bedroom. Tita warned, "If you're not scared now, you will be when you hear their cracking sound." The whips looked evil. I wondered what they had to do with moaning. And why should I be scared?

The *chicotes* consisted of a wooden handle and braided strips made of yucca leaves. Such yucca plants were not grown anywhere near my *abuelos'* home. I had never seen whips such as these. I knew they would not be used on animals because of how delicate they looked. I also couldn't understand why they would be hung alongside pictures of saints inside the house.

Come to think about it, I realized that I had seen the same yucca whips hanging inside some of our other friends' houses too. Rampo owned a whip, but his was made of leather and hung in the tack house. He would snap his whip above the horses' backs and shout for them to get moving, but he never actually hit them with it. He was a kind man.

Tita, who was thick into her storytelling, interrupted my thoughts. "When you go to the services, it will be so dark, you won't be able to see your hand, even if you hold it right in front of your face." I couldn't imagine how dark that must be. There was always some light at my *abuelos'* house. Just with the stars at night, I could see my hands and feet. Even on the darkest of nights, the votive candle that resided on Nanita's altar with all her favorite statues of the saints provided some light.

Tita was really enjoying trying to scare me, knowing that I would be attending services at *la morada* for the first time. Although I had never been to a *Penitente* chapel, I could not admit that I was scared. My *abuelos* prepared Junior and me for weeks about the *Penitente* members and their rituals. They wanted us to know as much as possible before our first experience.

At the end of each lesson, Nanita would say, *"Hijitos, si van a tener miedo, no vamos. Está bien con Rampo y conmigo. Hemos ido muchas veces. Nos podemos quedar y rezar juntos, solo nuestra familia, el Jueves Santo."* My children, she said, if you are going to be scared, we won't go. It's really okay with Rampo and me. We have gone many times before. We can stay home and pray together on Holy Thursday, just our family.

But I wanted her to know that I was brave. I told her, *"¡Nanita! Junior y yo no tenemos miedo. Nosotros queremos ir. Queremos rezar con todos."* Although I assured her that Junior and I were not scared and wanted to go pray with everyone, inside, I was trembling. And it was only Monday.

In the town of Las Vegas, almost everyone looked forward to Easter. Our neighbors would decorate their homes with bunnies, yellow daffodils, and tulips. Parents would take their children to the Five and Dime Store to buy the cutest, most ornate Easter baskets. All the eggs in the grocery store would be bought and colored for a big Easter egg hunt on Sunday.

In my *abuelos'* community, Easter egg hunts were unheard of and bunnies were caught for eating. Instead, we celebrated *La Semana Santa*, the Holy Week before Easter, and then went to mass to celebrate the resurrection of Jesus on Easter Sunday. The *Penitentes Cofradía de Nuestro Padre Jesús,* the Religious Members of the Brotherhood of Our Lord Jesus Christ, who everyone called *Los Hermanos* for short, led many of the rituals during the holy week.

Rampo explained that the *Penitentes* had served the people of northern New Mexico and southern Colorado with ancient Catholic practices for over 400 years. The reason, he said, was that when this part of the country was owned by Spain, there was a shortage of priests in the area, and so the *Penitentes* devoted themselves to keeping the Catholic faith alive. They also continued the Catholic practice of helping their communities with acts of charity. But they were criticized since the Catholic Church, at that time, did not appreciate the ancient religious dramas held during Holy Week, especially acting out how Jesus was whipped as he carried a big wooden cross to Mount Calvary. Later in the twentieth century, the Catholic Church came to better understand the deep spiritual meaning of reenacting the crucifixion and accepted how it helped to keep people faithful to the Church.

The members of the *Penitentes* who I knew were wonderful, caring men. They helped anyone down on their luck, even though they were all very poor themselves. They were all-around Good Samaritans, assisting families in whatever was needed. When a death was involved, they prayed the rosary at wakes before a funeral. We learned from our *abuelos,* that *El Hermano Mayor* was in charge of the whole organization of Penitentes and all the ceremonies. He was a good friend of my *abuelos* and often visited our home. I liked his quiet ways.

The other *Penitentes* had other tasks to do during the services. *El Rezador* read from an old prayer book and led the *oraciones.* After each prayer, members would respond in unison with longer prayers. Our *abuelos* assured us that the *Penitentes* had memorized these long responses. In between these *oraciones*, we were told to expect the *Penitentes* to sing at the top of their lungs in a very devoted, spiritual way. These sorrowful Spanish hymns were called *alabados*.

By the time I got back home from Tita's house and her terrifying stories, I was full of questions. Was it true that inside *la morada* it was pitch dark? How were the whips going to be used? Would the whip be used on me? Did I need to know all the prayers and sing the songs? What if I didn't know them? Would other children be there too?

I knew, however, that it was not my place to ask Rampo more about the services. I also assumed that he wouldn't be able to answer my questions to relieve my fear. Because he was not originally from Las Manuelitas, Rampo had never been a member of the *Penitentes*. The *Hermanos* were full of secrets, so they wouldn't have told him anyway.

I had to stop worrying. Despite my fear of what was to come, I was still fascinated with everything related to *Los Hermanos.* Besides, we had enough of our own traditions during Holy Week to make up for not knowing theirs. After completing our chores each day, we prayed the rosary on our knees in front of Nanita's altar. It was a very solemn week: no singing, dancing, or playing games was allowed.

When Holy Thursday arrived, I was ready for the upcoming events; I was still afraid, but ready. We did the same chores and had our meals at the usual time, but we prayed even more than we had all week long. After supper, Nanita asked me, *"Hijita, esta es tu última oportunidad para decir si quieres ir o no. ¿Estás lista para decirme?"* She gave me one last chance to avoid going.

Las Tinieblas was the religious service where the *Penitentes* enacted the events of Palm Sunday up to Jesus' burial. And boy, was I ready! My fear had been mostly overcome through the praying we had done during the week and the religious way it made me feel. I replied with an enthusiastic, *"¡Sí!"* Junior and I quickly went to wash up and change into clean clothes. Nanita then brushed my hair until it shone and put pretty bows on my long braids. Rampo got out the wagon, harnessed the horses, and off we went to *la morada* further up the valley.

There were many people already there when we arrived, including our *compadres* and *comadres*. Horse-pulled wagons were lined up along the road and in the field close to *la morada*. Like all gatherings, people were busy greeting one another and catching up on the news. Individuals and small groups would eventually go into *la morada* and pray for a while and come back out.

La morada was the *Penitentes'* private chapel. The small adobe building was built with one side door, but no windows. Next to the entrance of the chapel door was a small room. Nanita told me that only members of the *Penitentes* were allowed to enter. I could not take my eyes away from the door of that secret room. What could be in there?

We finally went into the chapel and knelt next to the open entrance door to pray. I knew the Penitente members were in their secret room and, despite my desire to concentrate on my prayer, I was sidetracked by my curiosity. I bowed my head, but my eyes would creep open to sneak a look outside toward the closed door. I strained my eyes and imagined that I could see through the cracks in the heavy wooden door. I imagined that I had x-ray vision.

Someone entered the *Penitentes'* room and my heart started pounding as the door was left ajar. I turned my head a little more to see if I could get a better view. It was very dark inside. All I could see was the brown adobe walls and dirt floors.

I was so obsessed trying to look inside the *Penitentes'* room, that it took me totally by surprise when the chapel door creaked and banged closed. I nearly fell off the pew! There was absolutely no light: Tita was right! I could not see my hands.

Nanita calmed me by gently taking one of my hands and holding it in her own. It was her silent signal that I was safe. But even the safety net of her hand was weakened when next I heard the chapel door creak open followed by the footsteps of men slowly shuffling into the room. As they walked in a single file, I remembered Nanita telling me that they would be representing Jesus Christ and his twelve disciples.

The room was tiny, suffocating. As the candles were lit on the front altar, Nanita whispered, asking me if I was okay, "*¿Estás bien?*" I reassured her, whispering back, "*Sí, estoy bien.*"

The candles offered pinpricks of light, but did nothing to chase away the blackness. I found myself staring at the flames and then turning my eyes away to see the crazy designs my eyes would make as they accustomed themselves to the black. This game didn't last long because the loud chanting of the sorrowful *alabados* began.

I remembered then what Rampo had told me: *Alabados* were ancient Spanish hymns about life, death, and devotion. The *Penitentes* used a longer name for these chants, *Alabado sea Dios*, praised be God, or *Alabado sea el Señor*, praised be the Lord.

The *alabados* lasted a long time, but I did not mind the haunting melody. It was enchanting. The grieving voices hypnotized me as I imagined the agony of what had happened to Jesus Christ the day after the Last Supper.

After the *alabados* ended, all was quiet, and then one candle at a time was snuffed out. As each candle was extinguished, a long prayer was said in the same mournful and passionate way as in the earlier chants. I could smell the last smoky traces of each candle as tiny specks of light struggled to survive, then disappeared.

Finally, one remaining candle was left burning to represent Jesus Christ. It seemed to glow with a distinct halo. The tone of the chants changed once again. The voices of the *Penitentes* now turned into weeping, sorrowful cries. My eyes filled with tears as I was overtaken with sadness and an empty feeling of loss.

I was so spellbound by the prayers and ceremony of the candles that I almost jumped out of my skin when the light representing Jesus Christ suddenly went out. At the exact moment, a deafening noise commenced. Chains of metal rattled, a very large, wooden *matraca* shook, and the men's cries intensified and turned feverish.

It took only a moment to realize that their cries came, not just from how they were singing, but also from actual pain. I had not been able to see them in the darkness, but the men were holding a different whip called *la disciplina*. These whips were a shorter version of the *chicote* and easier to use in a small crowded space like the tiny *morada*. It was the *disciplinas* that changed the tone of their laments: Now, in the midst of the racket, I heard the strands of *amole* fibers cut through the air and make contact with the men's backs.

I knew they couldn't be hitting their backs very hard because they had to hit themselves over the shoulder, but the strands of *amole* were razor sharp and could hurt. As their moans began to increase, a flute began playing weeping notes. I could almost see the notes floating through the air like an angel, and I felt a lifeline coming directly from heaven.

I was no longer afraid. As suddenly as the noise started, it stopped. The silence reminded me to breathe. As if on cue, the chants began anew. The candles were not relit. The men no longer whipped their backs. When the powerful chanting resumed, they filled me with deep sorrow.

In that moment, I understood why the men would choose to cause pain to themselves. They wanted to share the journey with Jesus Christ during the crucifixion. Although I had not felt the physical pain, I felt myself no longer standing in an adobe chapel holding Nanita's hand. I was actually there with Jesus Christ. I heard the whip slice through the air. I heard it hit his back and heard his painful groan. It was totally real, and I was there. I never experienced so much sorrow in my short life as I did that first time at *Las Tinieblas*.

After what seemed an eternity, the chapel door flung open and the candles were lit again. More praying and singing followed before the congregation filed out into a black night filled with glowing stars and a bright moon. We, *los feligrezes*, were quiet and sad. No one among the congregation dared speak. There was not a single joyful exchange.

We children climbed onto the wagon for the trip home, and, wrapped in Nanita's quilts, immediately fell asleep. We were totally exhausted, emotionally drained, and knew that this experience would live with us forever.

Chapter 11: Mysterious Chanting

Good Friday was to be another memorable day, and an even more memorable night.

On Good Friday we returned to *la morada* for another solemn ceremony. As we waited outside, a *comadre* came up to Nanita to give her a hug, to share the sadness of Good Friday, and to ask after the family. She said, "*El Viernes Santo siempre es un día tan triste, pero ¿Qué vamos a hacer, comadre? ¿Todo está bien con su familia?*"

Nanita said, "*Sí, gracias a Dios. Oí que Eduardo se fué para Colorado. ¿Sabes si ya llegó?*" Nanita responded with news that she had learned earlier that morning, asking whether her *comadre* knew if Eduardo had arrived safely in Colorado.

The *comadre* replied, "*Sí, ya llegó. Está en la casa de mi comadre Aurora.*" He had indeed arrived at the house of her *comadre*.

All conversations stopped as soon as the *Penitentes* arrived and commenced with the Stations of the Cross. Fourteen crosses were erected across the green meadow from *la morada*. Each cross was draped in soft purple material that waved sorrowfully like sheets on a clothesline billowing in a soft wind. The entire group of churchgoers followed behind the *Penitentes,* chanting and praying along the way. Old and young knelt down, stood up, and knelt down again at each prayer station, whether they were on grass or weeds.

At the center of our prayer line, a man carried a heavy, roughly hewn wooden cross that was large enough to have been used in a real crucifixion. The cross bearer carried the entire weight himself on one shoulder with his arms wrapped around it to keep it from slipping. Each year, one man is given the honor of carrying this brutally heavy cross.

The cross bearer wore a white hood, so we could not see his face, and was naked from the waist up. Two other *Penitentes* walked alongside him and lashed his back and their own with the *chicote* as they journeyed along the path. The deep abrasions on their backs formed a red and swollen symbol of their sacrifice. When the first *Penitente* tired, one of the other two would take the cross and continue walking. As we followed them, my brother and I sidestepped the marks made in the ground where they dragged the cross as if the marks were sacred and should not be marred by footprints.

As the *Penitentes* continued walking, they prayed, sang, and moaned just as they had the night before in *la morada*. Being in an open field, instead of in the tightly sealed cramped room of the night before, lessened the intensity. A single cloud of dust arose from the shuffling of feet mixed with the smell of crushed weeds and human sweat as we moved to each station in the scorching sun.

Most of the women were dressed in black with their faces mostly covered with heavy, black-fringed *tápalos*. There was no shade or relief, just the feeling of discomfort. But ours was mild compared to what the cross-bearing *Penitentes* must have felt. Occasionally, the assistants would wipe the brow of the cross-bearer with what looked like a damp cloth.

When the praying at the Stations of the Cross was over, the cross bearer turned to us and held the cross upright. We all immediately knelt and began a series of prayers honoring the death of Jesus Christ. The *Hermano Mayor* led us through the Hail Mary, the Our Father, and other prayers that I did not know, but mumbled along as if I knew them.

At exactly 3:00 pm, as if determined by centuries of practice, the prayers stopped and there was total silence. This hour was the time Jesus was believed to have died on the cross. The abrupt silence was troubling and very unsettling. I didn't hear a bird chirp and the slight breeze that had helped cool my face stopped dead still. A feeling washed over me, as I am sure it did over everyone else, that we were experiencing the death of Jesus for the first time.

When the ceremony closed, the community remained silent and respectfully slipped away to their waiting wagons. The *Penitentes,* silent for the first time, proceeded into *la morada*. I have no idea what came next because this was one of their secret moments that we were not allowed to see. It didn't matter to me. I was completely drained of energy from the long, emotional week. I was ready to go home and climb under one of Nanita's colorful quilts for solace and rest.

The night was to hold one more sacred experience.

As we arrived at the *ranchito*, a light dusting of spring snow had fallen, but the night had cleared. The moon was huge and illuminated everything. We all went straight to bed and to sleep. At midnight, loud chanting woke us. It sounded to us like the *alabados* that were sung earlier in the service.

My *abuelos* had also heard the singing. Nanita came to our beds and told us to bundle up before going outside into the cold. We quickly dressed to see what was happening. My *abuelos* thought someone was coming to the house, so we stood waiting on the *portal*, listening to the distant chant. Then we realized that the chanting was coming from the mountain behind the *ranchito*. We started to walk in that direction. Rampo whispered to us to go only as far as a nearby hill.

I will never forget what we saw. With the full moon in the background, we could see the silhouettes of the *Penitentes* walking in a single file on the mountain ridge we called *El Crestón*. The leader carried a cross and all sang their haunting songs of lament, which chilled us even more than the icy ground on which we were standing. I was reminded of the Stations of the Cross. Rampo and Nanita led us in prayers until the last silhouette disappeared. They said they did not know the words to the hymns, but we could join in their sacrifice by praying. Without question we went down on our knees, ignoring our now soggy clothes, and began to pray.

¿Quién en esta casa da luz? Jesús;
¿Quién la llena de alegría? María;
¿Y quién le da fe? José;
Luego bien claro se ve que siempre
habrá contrición teniendo en el Corazón,
a Jesús, María, y José. Amén.

Who gives light to this house? Jesus;
Who fills it with joy? Mary;
And who gives it faith? Joseph;
Then clearly you can see that there
always will be contrition kept in the heart
for Jesus, Mary, and Joseph. Amen.

Returning home, we reflected on what we had just experienced. The midnight walk of the *Penitentes* was unfamiliar to even our *abuelos*. Nanita lit a fire in the stove and heated some hot milk for us to drink before we went back to bed. The next morning, we walked to the white wooden cross that Rampo had built on top of a *mesa* farther away from the house than where we had been the previous night. Nothing prepared us for what we were to see.

To our surprise, we saw spots of blood around the base of the cross. The drops led into the forest of *pinos*, but Rampo said, "*No vamos más allá. Esto es privado y sagrado. Debemos respetar su adoración y sacrificio privado.*" To him, it was important that we stop, for we should respect the privacy of their worship and sacrifice. We did not go any further.

We willingly left the cross and drops of blood in the snow behind and tucked away in our minds the events of the evening before, considering it a special privilege that we had been honored to witness. Saturday came and went, and we completed our chores as usual; but Nanita added extra prayers to our normal list of Catholic mantras. I felt like I was in a trance all day and in a special way closer to God.

On Easter Sunday we awoke early to travel by wagon to our beloved Catholic church in Sapelló. Everyone was there, but nobody asked those of us who were missing from the Lenten events why we had been absent. They knew about *Las Tinieblas* and respected those who participated.

The next day, I went to play at Tita's house. I was eager to make it known to her that I had not been scared. Nanita stood on her *portal* keeping me in sight until I got there. The deafening commotion of the neighbors' many dogs was a dead giveaway that I had arrived safely. When I called every dog by name, they cheerfully escorted me to the house with tails wagging.

Tita and her siblings met me at the door and we went inside to play. Tita's dad was always very kind and warm to me. Today we were told to be quiet because he did not feel well. That was rare; he was always out and about on his property tending to his many chores. I asked what was wrong, and his wife replied that it looked like he had a cold.

We played in the kitchen for a long time, and then one of the girls opened the door into the next room to get something we needed. I followed her and saw her dad on the bed. Since I knew him well, I went over and put my arms around him as I always did and said, "*Buenos Días.*" This time he yelled when I gave him my usual bear hug. I jumped away, and his wife came running and scolded us for being in the room. She quickly chased us out, but I could not forget his painful shout. He did not even return my warm hello.

Nanita came about three o'clock to visit and take me home. She and Tita's mother talked about her husband's's *heridas.* I was curious about the wounds on his back, but had been told never to interfere in adult conversation, so I said nothing.

On the way home, Nanita told me something my little ears had never expected to hear. Tita's father was the *Penitente* who had portrayed Jesus Christ; his back was still very sore from what he had endured during Holy Thursday and Good Friday. At that moment, I realized how much the *Hermanos* sacrificed as *Penitentes* to keep the faith of our community strong.

Fun Pursuits

Chapter 12: Adventures with Dick and June

Junior and I looked forward to chores at the *ranchito*.

Our chores included helping with house cleaning, washing vegetables, sweeping the front patio, caring for the animals, fetching wood, and bringing water in buckets from the well. Yes! These were achingly dull tasks. We, however, always found ways to make them more exciting than our *abuelos* had planned. "*¡Vamos!*" we'd shout. Let's go! was our *grito* as we raced to the next chore of the hour.

Exercising the male workhorses was one of our favorite chores. Dick and June were huge, heavy, and good-natured beasts. We were lucky they let us do anything we wanted to them. Dick was docile and stood still for us in the middle of the field until we learned how to straddle him; it took a dozen times before we finally succeeded. June was not so willing to stand still for us. We had to push and pull him to a nearby fence from which we could jump on his back.

We first learned to ride Dick and June bareback. Rampo led them down the path and we bounced with each step they took. With a little practice, we learned to saddle and mount them by ourselves. When riding the horses, Junior and I would sometimes spontaneously dismount our horses and immediately remount them to show off that we no longer needed to coax them to a fence post or pull on them to get into the saddle.

One thing we never got to do was bridle the horses. Their heads were too big for us to put the reins over their necks. Even Nanita had a difficult time trying to get them on, so that chore was reserved for Rampo. We didn't feel too bad about not being able to help with that task. It was darn hard!

Sometimes when the fields were freshly plowed, and the dirt formed uneven mounds, Rampo would harness what looked like a big heavy board to Dick and June. Junior and I would be told to sit on the center of the board to weigh it down. We were helping to flatten the loose dirt, but what fun it was to bounce up and down behind the big horses! Nanita intensely disliked that we be covered with dust from head to toe. As punishment for enjoying getting so dirty, Nanita told us to bathe in the creek with the horses. But bathing in the creek was just another amusement for us!

Late one afternoon, Junior and I were riding on June with our legs barely reaching his sides. My brother was guiding June sitting on the saddle, and I was sitting behind him on June's rump. We were headed toward the creek's edge. It was full of tall trees, bushes, and lots of wild flowers.

Unexpectedly, June neighed and reared up on his hind legs. We both fell off the horse and landed on our rears, just as a *gato montez* dashed into the bushes. We were unhurt, but terrified of the puma and June was acting wild. Getting water at the nearby well, Nanita heard the commotion. She cautiously ran toward us and yelled at June to settle down. She was afraid that we might be hurt and that the *gato montez* would return to attack us. Thank goodness the enormous cat did not return. Only our pride was wounded for not being able to stay on June.

As the summer lengthened, Junior and I learned to handle the horses and began racing them. In fact, we got pretty good at competing against the local kids who had ridden bareback since they were babies. One day as we returned to the *ranchito* from the grocery store, we noticed a group of neighbor children riding a couple of skinny, spirited horses near Rampo's fields. We asked Mamita if we could join them with Dick and June. She agreed, but we had to change our outfits and put on our most ragged, washed out, and patched clothes that were reserved solely for playing or doing our chores.

I quickly changed and joined the group before my brother caught up with me. While greeting everyone, I noticed there was an older boy who I did not know. When he saw me walking with June, he smirked, *"Estos chicos de la ciudad son grandes, pero no saben como montar los caballos."* When I heard him say, those town kids, even if they are big, they don't know how to ride horses, I fell for the bait.

I replied, *"¡O! Yo puedo montar y probablemente mejor que tú."* After giving this challenge that I could ride better than him, the race was on. He held the saddle while I got on and then he handed me the reins. Darn nice of him.

In a blink of an eye, I spurred June into a fast gallop. All anyone could see was a big dust cloud as I took off. I raced to the end of the road, turned June and rode back as fast as I could. As I neared the group, I could see the group clapping and cheering for me. Not surprising, the new boy stood quiet. This was an exciting event since few girls were included in the group, and even fewer girls met a boy's taunts and challenges.

As I started to dismount, the saddle came tumbling down, and the boy who had egged me on said, "*Estos chicos de la ciudad. Son tan grandes y ni siquiera saben como ensillar un caballo.*" When he made fun of me for not knowing how to saddle a horse, I knew what had happened. Unbeknownst to me, he had loosened my horse's cinch belt, but I had shown him and not fallen off. I felt proud of myself. Not only did I not fall, it was the fastest I had ever ridden a horse.

I loved June even more after that incident. I was glad Nanita and Rampo had not seen me racing. Or had they?

Chapter 13: Our Pet Menagerie

Rampo and Nanita's *ranchito* was like a petting zoo.

In addition to Dick and June, my *abuelos* had a menagerie of animals at the *ranchito*. We considered them our friends. And oh! They all had English names which I'm sure we kids probably pronounced incorrectly. But, we were not alone. The grownups butchered these names too.

June was with the family for many years. When Dick died of old age, he was replaced with a more spirited horse named Whitey. Although he was a heavy work horse, he did not put up with our wanting to ride him. He was always baring his teeth and trying to bite us even though we fed him lots of apples. He was not the friendly sort. Whitey did not last long and was soon replaced with a calmer horse named Don.

Rampo and Nanita always had a dog around to take care of us. When we were at the *ranchito*, Nanita would point to the poor dog and admonish him by saying, "*Cuídalos.*" Because the dog was told to take care of us, we knew the dogs were there for us grandchildren. Nanita and Rampo acquired a new dog several times during the summers I visited them. Sometimes it was Papito who brought them a dog. Stray dogs hung around his shoe shop and he would feed them scraps. When one stayed too long, he brought it out to the *ranchito.* Papito named the dogs after items he had in his shoe shop. These were unlikely names for dogs, especially for Spanish speakers. For example, when I was about six or seven years old, Nanita and Rampo had a dog named Bolts, like the metal nuts and bolts. We added an "e" to his name, calling him, *Bolte*. He was a mixed breed that looked as though lots of German shepherd blood ran through his veins. He followed us everywhere and acted as our chaperone. Everywhere we went, he showed up. He was playful and often knocked us over in his eagerness to lick us and stay close. We loved him and wished he could come indoors. However, that was taboo: no animals were allowed in the house. Dogs were meant to protect the family, the farm animals, and the house from unwanted intruders.

The only animal that got to come inside was a black and white furry cat. This big, non-descript cat was not allowed on the furniture, and had to stay out of the kitchen. He obeyed Nanita whenever she called him by his Spanish name of *Gatito*. I do not know how Nanita trained him, but he pretty much obeyed the house rules. We kids called him by his English name of Kitty Cat.

After Bolts died, my *abuelos'* next dog was a small, black terrier called Rivet. He loved to jump high and knock down Junior and I whenever he had a chance. Rivet was a bundle of energy. You often would hear us, between gales of laughter, "No, No, Rivet, stay down," but Rivet did whatever he pleased.

The last dog they had was named Nuts. He was not crazy; his name matched with the first dog. The pair was Nuts and Bolts. This dog was the ugliest, most playful little mongrel you ever saw. We adored him, and he was crazy in love with us.

There was only one lonely cow, a white and brown jersey. Her name was Brownie. I tried so hard to learn how to milk poor Brownie. Nanita made it look easy, but if I finally got the milk going, the stream would miss the bucket, or the darn cow would move, or I would fall off the stool and tip the milk bucket. I guess Rampo never learned either; I never saw him milk the cow. Sometimes I wondered if he viewed this as a woman's job.

When Nanita was milking, she would give us hot, foamy milk in tin cups. We would get white moustaches and would laugh loudly and spook the cow, so Nanita would make us go away. How was I supposed to learn how to milk if I couldn't watch Nanita? I never did learn.

We also had about a dozen chickens. They slept in a coop at night to be protected from the nocturnal animals. Vera named the birds. She called them Hedy Lamarr, Bette Davis, Betty Grable, and so on. Based on the chickens' names, I am sure our *abuelos* knew what magazines Vera was borrowing and who were her favorite movie stars.

In the daytime, the chickens were free and roamed everywhere. It was not unusual to miss a hen when gathering them for the night and these would roost in the trees until the next day. Junior and I were then given the job of finding the eggs, which could be under bushes or in grassy areas. Sometimes they laid them in plain sight, like on the dirt paths. We learned to listen for the sound of loud clucking. The chicken's cluck would tell us she had just finished laying an egg. When we missed finding an egg, we would soon see hatched baby chicks wandering in the weeds. Junior and I would run to play with them, but sometimes the mama hen or a rooster would chase us. We sometimes spooked them to make them squawk and fly away; then we could carefully sneak up behind the chicks and grab them. We loved cuddling the soft chicks, although their loud peeping drove us nuts.

As a child, I wondered if our *abuelos* had all these animals in order to feed us our favorite foods or just to keep us busy. The menagerie did take up much of our time while at the *ranchito* and it was hard work. But in reality, caring for the pet menagerie was fun and entertaining.

Chapter 14: A Tail in the Air

"*Ve más despacio.*"

I told Junior to go slower because, at my "advanced" age of eight, Junior still seemed so clumsy. The most incredible yellow butterfly had just landed on the head of a purple flower and I wanted to capture it.

We were in a lovely green meadow, which was down a small hill from the front porch and across the small *arroyo.* The meadow had flowers of all colors and varieties. It also was home to many beautiful birds. The yellow-breasted meadowlarks made their nests in the endless fields of green grass and the larks flitted around as they tweeted their delicate high-pitched songs. When we got too close to their nests, they would fly around our heads and try to lead us away from their chicks. We were on to them, but they were safe with us. All the adults in our family loved birds, and we were reminded not to scare the *pajaritos* away, for the birds are God's creatures.

Junior was sneaking up on a butterfly that had landed right beside me. He was so noisy; he didn't know how to walk silently and instead clumsily walked around me, stumbling over rocks and sticks. I just knew he was going to scare the gentle butterfly away.

Before Junior reached the butterfly, I turned slowly and raised my homemade net to capture it. The net was made from Nanita's cheesecloth and tied onto a willow stick. I was very proud of her handiwork, and Junior was not allowed to touch it. I was the oldest and Nanita left me in charge of the net.

"*¡Cuidado!*" Junior shrieked so loudly that I was sure the neighbors a mile away could hear him tell me to be careful. I snapped back, "*¡Silencio!*"

Just at that moment, a slight breeze came up and we both watched as the butterfly fluttered into the current and disappeared. That loss did not deter us. We were forever on the lookout for the next exciting thing to chase or catch. We went after anything that moved—anything that is, that did not scare us.

We put the unlucky butterflies into glass jars with holes in the lids for air. We filled the jars with grass and flowers for the butterflies to enjoy, and then we took the butterflies home to Nanita. They were our "live art." We would carry them around, put them up to the sunlight, and turn the jar around and around to look at their antennae, eyes, and the patterns on their wings. Nanita would let us put them on the windowsills or table in the evening so we could enjoy them a little longer before letting them go free the next morning.

Resigned that we weren't going to have this particular butterfly to take home to Nanita, we raced each other to the nearest tree. Something right on the edge of the meadow suddenly moved. As we neared the tree, Junior yelled at me to look, "*¡Mira, Mira!*"

I followed Junior's finger to where he was pointing and screamed with excitement. "*Es un zorrillo.*" Our pace never slowed as we veered towards the black and white tail sticking straight up among the tall grasses and wildflowers. The skunk's tail was waving at us and beckoning us to pet it.

As we neared the tail, we both sang out in unison, "*¡Que lindo!*" It's beautiful!, we said. We could now see the entire animal. He had black and white stripes, a shiny coat, a pointed face, and a bushy tail. As we ran toward him, he quickly sprinted on his stubby legs, keeping his tail raised.

We had been told many times to stay away from *zorrillos* because of their intolerable musky smell. We had driven by a dead skunk and experienced its nasty odor. But for some reason, this skunk did not seem to stink. The wild pink roses were blooming, and their overpowering fragrance was everywhere. Right there and then, Junior and I decided that the skunk would be more fun to catch than the butterflies. I imagined us catching the skunk and bringing him to the *ranchito* for Nanita. Maybe she would let him be our pet!

With that thought in mind, we began to follow the animal wherever he zigzagged. We encouraged him to move fast by yelling and trying to stampede him. As we pursued the skunk, I told Junior to split up, "*Vamos a separarnos.*"

Junior then loudly whispered, "*Vamos a ponerlo entre nosotros. Luego tú te vienes a la derecha y yo por la izquierda. Así no se puede escapar.*" He knew that we could get the skunk in between us if I came in from the right and he came in from the left.

We were able to reach out and almost touch his soft tail, but the animal was fast and always just a little ahead of us. I was so eager to catch him: I wanted to hug him and bury my face in his soft fur, like I would a puppy. At that moment, a fleeting thought of my *abuelos* saying that they smelled and that we should stay away from *zorrillos* darted through my mind, but this one was just fun and looked so soft. I could not smell anything but the fragrent meadow flowers.

Finally, the skunk seemed to tire of our game and took off to a nearby *arroyo*. He quickly slipped into a crevice between two big rocks and wiggled himself into it, but we knew where he was. As we peeked inside we could see the whites of his eyes in the little dark cave.

The skunk had been the best part of the whole afternoon and we wanted to keep chasing him. We looked for something to help us get him out and soon found a long stick. We then took turns poking and poking into the small dark crevice. That skunk was stubborn and wouldn't come out!

It was clear we were not going to catch him. Tired of poking into the cave, we crawled out of the *arroyo* and ran toward the house. We wanted to ask Nanita to help us get the skunk.

As we got closer to the house, we could see Nanita standing at the door. Her expression seemed to suddenly change to a scowl and she put her hands on her hips. We rarely saw her mad, but we could not grasp why she might be angry with us. She pinched her nose and hollered, "*¡Muchachos marranos! Huelen terrible.*" She continued screaming at us, "*¡Váyanse para el río de una vez y bañense! Yo les traigo ropa limpia.*" We couldn't understand why she called us dirty kids and told us that we smelled terrible, but we followed her instruction to go quickly to the creek for a bath.

"*¡Muchachos marranos!*" she muttered again under her breath and went back into the house now holding her nose and covering her mouth. We knew at that moment we were in deep trouble, but we still couldn't figure out what we had done wrong.

We ran as fast as our skinny legs would carry us to the creek. We took off our outer clothes and got into the cold, shallow water. Quickly we found another fun thing to do. We started splashing each other with glee. Our game ended when we heard Nanita yelling as she came to the creek, "*¿No se huelen, muchachos tontos?*" She didn't usually call us dummies, so we looked at each other, but we couldn't smell anything.

She was beside herself and bombarded us with questions: "*¿No saben lo que puede hacer un zorrillo? ¿Dónde vieron el zorrillo? ¿Por qué estaban tan cerca de él?*"

As we desperately tried to answer her non-stop list of questions – Don't you know what a skunk can do to you? Where did you see the skunk? Why did you get so close to him? – Nanita still held her nose. She then handed us a yellow bar of soap and placed our clean clothes on a rock. She told us to take off our undergarments and wash them thoroughly too. Nanita kept her distance.

Under her watchful eyes, we scrubbed and scrubbed until she said we could come out. After we were dressed, she still wasn't satisfied. She kept repeating how disgusted she was with how we smelled like a skunk and how the stink was all over us, saying, "*Todavía huelen como un zorrillo. El olor está por todo sus cuerpos.*"

As we started back up the road to the house, we carried our wet clothes and were red in the face with shame. "Nanita," I said meekly, "*Acabo de recordar que dejé mi red de mariposas al lado del refugio del zorillo. Necesito regresar y hagararlo antes de que se pierda.*" I wanted to go back for my butterfly net that I had left next to the skunk's hiding place.

Nanita let out another angry wail and shouted, *"No pueden ir allí por un mes. ¡Hediondos! No escuchan. Les dijimos que no se acercaran a los zorrillos."* Because we didn't listen and went close to the skunk, we would not be allowed back in the meadow for a month.

We hung our heads. As we started to climb the porch stairs, she stopped us from entering the house and said, *"¡Ay! No entren en mi casa. Se quedan afuera y su ropa también. Tengo que calentar el agua y tratar de quitarles el olor."* She would have to heat water and try to get the smell out of our clothes.

Heating water was quite an effort. She had to light a fire under the outside tub, which was behind the house and haul fresh water from the well. We could tell she was still mad as she did not even ask us to help her. We wondered if she would ever love us again.

By now Rampo had come out to the porch to see what the commotion was all about. He, too, smelled us, and instantly knew what the problem was, even after our long and torturous bath at the creek. He held his nose and I thought it strange that he was trying to hide his mouth at the same time. He pointed at us and declared, *"¡Aja! Encontraron un zorrillo. Ahora si son zorrillitos."*

When he called us little skunks, he started to laugh in his deep manly voice, despite Nanita's warning look that this was no laughing matter. She wanted him to be mad too, but he wasn't. He winked at us when she wasn't looking, and we knew at that moment that at least he still loved us.

After the water was heated, Nanita let us help wash the clothes that we had previously rinsed in the creek. We were then ordered to take hot baths and wash the second set of clothes we had just put on. We didn't know when this constant washing was ever going to stop. She told us to stay out in the open to air dry. At least that was good because we got to run around and play again.

At long last she agreed to let us sit on the porch, where we ate our dinner. It was late evening before she allowed us into the house and let us forget what a stupid thing we had done.

Once in bed for the night we whispered to each other about the day's events. Junior quietly said, "*Supongo que nos metimos en problemas hoy.*" We had indeed gotten ourselves into a mess that day.

I sighed and replied, "*Creo que sí. Nunca más podremos seguir un zorrillo. Necesitamos estar lejos de ellos. Supongo que no es tanto que el zorrillo huele, es porque nos hace oler a nosotros. ¡O! Y nunca más quiero bañarme.*"

We would never chase a skunk again. It wasn't so much that the skunk smells, as that they make us smell. Oh! And I never wanted to take another bath.

Chapter 15: Games We Played

With all the chores we had at the *ranchito*, you would think we had little energy or time to play.

But we never seemed to tire. When done with our chores, we invented our own games and modified the games we learned at school to fit our imagination.

While wandering through the woods, we picked wild tomatoes and pumpkins. We did not care if they were over ripe or under ripe. We picked what was available and piled them behind a wagon wheel, a big board, or a large box. We called these hiding places our barricades and the vegetables were our ammunition to throw at each other. Time Out was the name of this game because it reminded us of chase games we played during school recess; during my childhood, Time Out was definitely not a punishment.

Sometimes we played with the other neighbor kids in teams or just between Junior and me. When playing in teams, we chose a leader to shout out when to begin pelting each other. The attack continued until we ran out of our home-made bombs. After playing Time Out, we dashed to *las acequias* to clean ourselves before the grownups saw what a mess we had made of our clothes.

If the end of our work day was still sunny and warm, we chased lizards. This hunt was something we loved to do. The *lagartijas* were always scurrying around the *ranchito* and there were tons of them, both big and small. We hunted them up and down boulders, up and down ravines, and even up and down the high steps to the porch. They seemed to come out only when it was hot and sunny. On those days, we dripped with perspiration from the chase. Nanita would warn us to stop bothering them because they ate insects, even mosquitos. She would yell from her kitchen, *"Déjenlos, esos comen insectos, hasta los mosquitos."* But we couldn't stop ourselves. We were mesmerized by their frantic running movements and chased them like cats after a mouse.

When it got too hot, Nanita told us to slow down and play quiet games. She told us to name the plants around us. We liked this game because Nanita took time to play with us and helped us in the naming game. She also encouraged us to dry plants that we thought were particularly pretty, label them, and paste them on a piece of cardboard to use later when play-acting school.

I often got to be the teacher when playing school, especially if Vera was not around. The role of *maestra* gave me the opportunity to show off what I had learned at school. It meant using English since we never had a teacher that spoke Spanish; a teacher such as Miss Tamme, Miss Calvin, Miss Kane, Miss Boyd, or Miss Roiser spoke only English. Because our English was limited, you can be sure we sneaked in enough Spanish to make our play-school fun. We also made a stick to point and to gently smack at kids that misbehaved. Sadly, it was a little too much like real school.

When we tired of school, we pretended to own a grocery store. We created shelves from boxes, the stairs to the house or wherever we were and stocked them with empty cans, bottles, and empty boxes. The long, thin sticks were spaghetti, and the little round stones were beans. We made labels for our 'grocery' items and included the cost on everything. Small pebbles turned into pennies, medium pebbles were nickels, and larger pebbles were dimes. With our make-believe coins we practiced giving correct change, but never added tax.

If we had to stay in the house because of rain or cold, we played with our rag dolls and role-played different characters. We always pretended to be a mother, sister, or brother. This game was of not much interest to the boys, so we girls ended up playing mothers and cooing sweet nothings to our dolls. We loved fussing over our dolls, like our mothers and grandmothers did over their babies, and made them comfortable when we put them down to sleep.

When the weather warmed up, we played outside and set up a small table and chair or two under a tree and played an alternative of house. We pretended to cook in a make-believe kitchen and serve coffee and *bizcochitos* at the table. Sometimes our menus included mud pies and our dishes were acorn caps, of all sizes. The leaves, flowers, and little stones found around the *ranchito* were the items we used for food. To make house-playing more fun, we used sticks to draw an outline of an elaborate house floor plan on the dirt. Our homes usually had many rooms. We stepped into each room and pantomimed what we would do in that area. Everyone laughed and cheered. During the game, we added rooms until we couldn't use them all because we did not have enough kids to fill the house.

We also liked to make our own toys, especially since we never owned any store bought ones. Luckily, we had a lots of items to fuel our imagination as Rampo and Nanita believed that everything might be of use later. Sometimes we got help from family adults, but usually we were left to our own devices. We made great tractors and other pull toys using empty thread spools. We even made whistles from the reeds we found in the ditches. By blowing tunes through the reeds, we created beautiful music all around us, or so we thought.

Other games that further influenced our antics on the *ranchito* came from those we learned at school. Red River was one of those games I learned and eventually taught to many of the community kids. The teachers called it "Red Rover," but I called it Red River. English was not our first language, and we did not know that rover meant a wanderer. As a Spanish speaker, the word sounded more like the English word river. This word I understood!

To play Red River, we formed two lines like a *rio* and faced each other, while holding our team members' hands. Standing several feet apart, the first team called one player from the opposite team by shouting, "RRed RRiver, RRed RRiver, send Cunde (or another player) on over!" Whoever was called had to run as fast they could to the other line and try to break the chain of linked hands. If the running player broke the link, they could pick a player from the opposing side to join their team. If the link was not broken, the runner had to join the opposing team. The game ended when only one team player was left on the opposite side.

I usually chose to be at the tail end of the line because I noticed early on that the boys typically rushed the middle part of the line, but my arm hurt when my teammates tried to hold arms too tightly to keep the boys from breaking our line. I was a 'namby-pamby' when it came to aggressive types of competitive games.

However, when it came to running, look out! I could show off my sprinting skills in the school game called Run, Sheep, Run. To us, the name of the game sounded like *Ronsheeperron*, so that is what we called it. I did not mind if I was a sheep or a fox because I was the fastest runner and whichever side I played, I outran most of the boys, even when I was barefoot. While still somewhat shy, I loved hearing my name called over and over along with the cheering and clapping as I went after our opponents. Another favorite running game for me was Tag, because I could again outrun nearly everyone. As free as the wind, off I would go. No inhibitions! Did I say I was shy?

When we were tired of running, we played another school game called Statues and stood frozen for as long as we could or until we broke into gales of laughter. Sometimes we dropped on our knees because we couldn't keep the pose. We ended up in many outlandish positions. I am sure we could have qualified for a great circus act with our gymnastic moves or certainly as clowns!

When fewer kids visited us, Rampo let us borrow a rope he used on the *ranchito* to play jump rope. Unlike those at school, his rope was heavy to turn and the braids of the rope were hard and itchy, but once we got the rope going, three or even four of us could jump together at one time. When we missed a step, the rope would brush against our skin and burn our flesh. I usually got tangled in the rope and cried when that rope took a bite out of me. Still, it was worth it to have something to do with other kids.

At times, we played the school game of Spinning. Two of us held hands and swirled around until we got dizzy. Letting go, we stopped and fell to the ground, laughing. This spinning seemed to be a girl's game because the boys that joined us left quickly. They might have thought it was a dumb game.

We added many other school games to our outdoor activities such as Hopscotch, Ring Around the Rosy, and Round the Mulberry Bush. We taught these games to younger neighbor children too. For example, before it got too dark in the evenings, we played Hide-and-Seek. The youngest member of the group typically was chosen to be It; this child counted to ten while the others hid, and then had to search all around the *ranchito*. I felt sorry for the young kids and gave them hints how to find us. The ones who were found then got mad at me and usually called the game off. I could never understand why they were not as excited as I was to be found so we could play the game over again.

I can't remember who taught us marbles. It was considered mostly a boy's game, but girls could play if the boys let them. I had long, bony fingers that were just right for the shooters we used to knock our opponent's marbles out of the ring. I kept a favorite shooter at the *ranchito*. The neighbor boys always wanted to trade it for one of theirs, but I would not because it was my lucky piece. Being two years older than my brother probably helped me beat him at the beginning, but not for long. By age eight, with practice, he became a master marble player. Fortunately for me, that is when I turned ten and no longer wanted to play a boy's game. In fact, my interests started to switch to more grownup activities with Vera. However, I did keep my shooter for good luck.

A game we must have learned from the men in the community started when one of us would spontaneously yell, "*Vamos a jugar lanzamiento.*" Following the call to arms, a pitching competition got started. We pitched empty cans, heavy nails, rag balls, chunks of wood, sticks, stones, and even our saliva past some imaginary line. The winner of the game was the person who flung the object past the line drawn in the dirt. Only the cheering and the yelling broke the intense focus of our efforts during this game.

Rampo was a great influence in our most dare-devil games. One of my favorites was walking on empty tin cans. I thought they made me look tall like a grownup. Rampo taught Junior and I to loop heavy string or cord through two openings that we made on the top of the cans and to tie them to our shoes. It did not take long for us to fall off the cans and skin our knees after we bounced up and down for a minute or two. So, after much experimentation, we figured out that adding long thin ropes and holding on to these ropes made it easier to walk.

We got good at walking, bouncing, and even running short distances on the cans before we fell, tumbling like spinning tops onto the rocky soil. In those days, there was no protective gear of any kind, but luckily, we never broke a bone. We just dealt with the scratches and bruises – no big deal!

A more thrilling version of this game was walking and running on *zancos*, tall stilts that Rampo made for us. These long sticks had a wedge nailed into them where we could place our feet. As we got better and better, Rampo raised the wedges higher and higher. Every kid around seemed to own a pair and we played until Nanita warned us that it was dark and that we needed to put away our stilts, saying, "*Cuidado, se van a caer en lo obscuro. Ya traigan sus zancos.*"

Rampo also taught us how to play with the wooden spinning tops he handcrafted for us. We would level a plot of dirt and then spin the tops by the hour. I was a great spinner, but never learned how to spin my top on the crown of another top. Several of the neighborhood boys were able to do it, and I wanted to imitate that feat, but never could. When I tried, it would crack the crown and the top would break into two pieces. I had to be satisfied with keeping my top upright when spinning. Besides, Rampo made the tops and we were supposed to take good care of them.

One game that required some skill before we could play was rolling a rim with a stick. Rampo made a rim from old metal and dented it at a certain angle so we could push and guide the rim wherever we wanted it to go. We had lots of fun, but it did require practice. I often lost control of the rim. However, I loved to get my turn and try my best.

I did a little better when we rode inside of old car tires: I was so darn skinny that I fit perfectly inside them! Without Rampo's knowledge, we turned this game into a downhill race. Each of us would take turns riding inside the tires with others pushing us down a hill. Most of the racers fell out early in the race, but I could stay in the tire for the longest period, enduring the painful bumping and jostling. The hardest part of this game was pushing the empty tires back up the rocky hill for another race. It was exhilarating going downhill, even if sometimes I got bruised when tossed out.

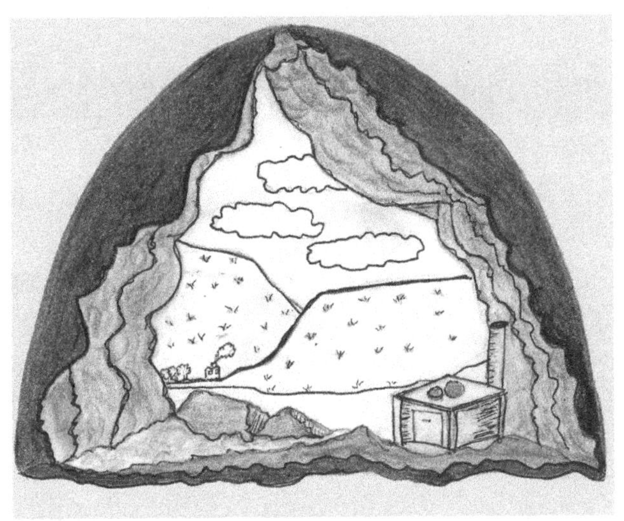

Chapter 16: Discovering a Hidden Treasure

What an honor! I felt like such a grownup.

On one clear day, Vera and our two cousins, Frances and Lily, allowed me to walk with them up the *mesa* behind our *abuelos'* house. Before we left the house, we were cautioned not to go beyond the property our *abuelos' ranchito*. I think mostly the adults wanted to keep an eye on us and to be able to hear us if we called.

I don't recall why I was allowed to tag along with the older girls. I was much younger, still a preteen, and not always welcome when the teenagers were together. Maybe it was because I was now taller than them, although still skinny and gangly.

Waving goodbye, we all ran up the mountain side, giggling as we shared make-believe adventures about who we were and what we were doing. The few movies we had seen helped set the stage for our roles as great explorers. We saw an occasional Western, so in our imagination we went to places no one had been to before, we caught wild mustangs, we were great ropers, we tamed horses, we caught bad guys! We played out all these fantasies as we moved along up the mountain.

We crossed the dirt road that ran across the *ranchito* and quickly reached the bottom of the mountain canyon. The entrance looked like a wide, deep *arroyo*. The sides were covered with fallen boulders and lots of pebble-like stones. Weeds and small bushes were nestled at the bottom of the small gorge.

Our destination was the top of the mountain, so we started climbing up the canyon. As I looked down, I could see the canyon becoming narrower and narrower. We were getting close to the top when we spotted what looked like a large cave. We started running toward the entrance, but weren't prepared for what we were about to see. As our sight adjusted to the darkness, we jumped and screamed with excitement. We couldn't believe the treasure in front of us. We had found it in the wilderness all by ourselves, and it was on "our" land.

The first thing we noticed was the bottom part of a black wood stove. It was set up at the end of the cave and had an upright stovepipe. The iron hot plates usually placed on top of the stove had been removed, as well as the hot water tank. Sitting next to the stove was the most interesting prize. We saw bags and bags of sugar and corn. We thought we were dreaming – all that sugar!

As we wandered around the cave inspecting the other objects, we commented on the strange odor, a smell none of us had ever experienced. It was something like wet, fermented corn. There were also piles of ashes all over the place. It seemed that poor stove was overworked. Not looking where I was going, I stumbled on a box of glass jars and lids. Luckily nothing broke.

It was very difficult to inventory all that we saw, especially with all our yelling and screaming. This day was better than a make-believe movie; this was a real life discovery! There were several tin buckets, pots, kettles, and even a big copper urn. Pipes and coils were strewn everywhere. We even found a wooden trough and some empty barrels on the ground.

When we finally came to our senses, we started asking ourselves, "*¿De quién será estas cosas? ¿Y, qué hacen aquí?*" We needed to know who owned these things and what they were making.

We couldn't figure it out, but our second eldest cousin, Frances, came up with a fantastic idea. Instead of worrying about the questions, she suggested we make fudge with the sugar. All she needed was cocoa.

After returning to the house that evening, someone stole the cocoa from Nanita's kitchen. I was sure she would be saved from going to hell because she would be able to go to confession the following Sunday and ask the priest to forgive her sin. Two of us secretly swiped two spoons and my sister took matches and a pot. While pretending to play outside, we hid our items in the bushes away from the house.

We could hardly sleep with the anticipation of knowing what we planned for the next day. We four girls all slept in the living room on the Murphy bed and kept whispering about our discovery and upcoming project. We must have been rather loud because Nanita told us to be quiet and go to sleep. We could hardly wait for the soft, morning light to appear in the sky.

After breakfast the next day and after quickly helping Nanita with the many household chores, we ran off on our much-anticipated trek to the cave, carrying our previously concealed supplies.

Sure enough, Frances made fudge without a recipe. The result was a sticky, syrupy concoction that never hardened, but we ate more than enough to make us sick. The day flew by and we knew we needed to head home.

No one wanted to leave the fudge behind, so we wrapped what was left in small pieces of paper that we found near the sacks of sugar. It was not very sanitary, but we needed something to hide the evidence and keep our secret. We dutifully stopped by the ditch and washed the utensils and hid them again. In the evening we would smuggle them back into the house.

When we reached the house, our *abuelos* greeted us and wanted to know what we had done and seen. We weren't used to lying, so it was a real chore not to be forthcoming. Thinking we had gotten away without mentioning our escapade, we started to go into the house. Then Lily accidentally dropped a packet of fudge from her pocket. Nanita picked it up, took one look at it, and calmly but firmly asked us to explain ourselves.

The whole story gushed out of us. We all talked at the same time, but somehow, we were able to tell what we had seen and done over the preceding two days. We spared no details. I felt so relieved and was sure we wouldn't have to explain our hijinks during our next confession, just our sins for stealing from Nanita.

Our *abuelos* were shocked beyond belief. Rampo seldom lost his temper, but this time he was close to it. He drilled us on every detail. Finally, when we were finished, he told us we had found a *destiladora* for making *mula* or moonshine. This still for making alcohol, he said, was a serious offense and it was against the law to have one. What made Rampo really mad was that it was on his property; he could be sent to jail. He was really upset and red-faced. He told us to immediately take him to see the *basurero*. When he called the still a trash pile, we knew he was angry.

Off we went following the same path we had walked for the past two days. Even Nanita joined us. Right then we knew the find was a very serious matter. When we arrived, Rampo studied the entire scene carefully. He walked through it all, stopped to look at us, and then said in a serious tone, "*Ustedes saben que no deben tocar y usar cosas que no son suyas. Le hemos enseñado a respetar las cosas de otras personas.*" Of course we knew better than to touch and use things that were not our own. We bowed our heads and felt remorse for not having shown respect. He added that the *federales* could come at any time, and these state police could accuse him of breaking the law because the *mula* still was on his land. That seemed to be the worst point.

The next morning, bright and early, we all went in Rampo's car to the grocery store in Sapelló. That was the place where men met to talk when they would go for groceries and gasoline. They usually drank an orange or red soda pop, as they shared information or gossiped.

When Rampo walked in, he turned to the men and told them in a very agitated, loud voice about the *mula* still he had found on his property. He added that he was going to have to tell the *alguasiles*, the sheriff deputies, because setting up and operating a *destiladora* was against the law. He asked if anyone knew to whom it belonged, but no one spoke up. He reminded them that if the ones who had built the still were caught, they would be imprisoned in *la Tuna*.

With that, we bought our groceries and left the store in silence. The men spread Rampo's message like a hot wind. Two days later, we walked back to the cave and found that every trace of the supplies was gone. Even the grounds were carefully raked and swept, just like when I swept the patio.

Rampo was pleased it was gone, but he wondered aloud over and over who could have set it up. We children, however, wondered how they had gotten the stove and supplies up and down the mountain. There were no roads, not even well-raked foot paths, just the brown canyon with the *arroyo*.

The next time we made fudge, it was with a recipe in Nanita's kitchen. We didn't have to hide the leftovers in our pockets. We didn't have to hide in a cave to make something special.

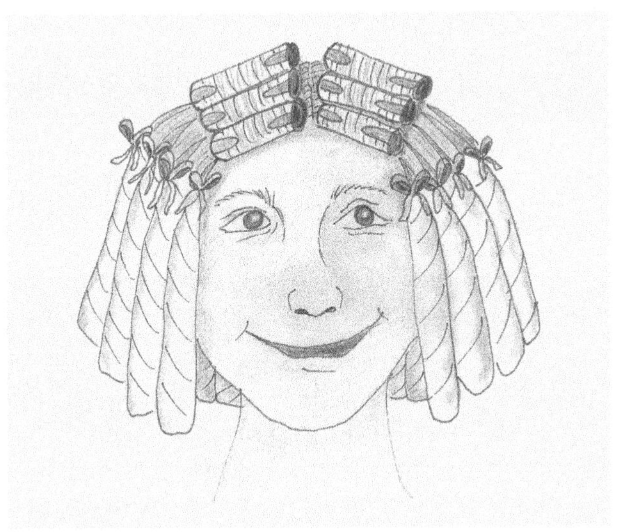

Chapter 17: The Ultimate Game

I so wanted to be like Vera.

She had wavy hair and always looked so stylish. My hair, on the other hand, was straight as a ruler and I usually wore childish looking braids with big, bright bows at the end. I was told that to look like Vera and the other adult women in my life, I would have to undergo the torture of curlers. I accepted the challenge!

In fact, I had to undergo two curling procedures. First came the hand-made curlers that Nanita created out of strips from coffee can lids and leather. These curlers created the ringlets I desperately wanted for my bangs, but they were not comfortable for sleeping. After curling my bangs, Nanita would remind me that all this trouble was required to be beautiful, saying, "*Todo para estar bonitas.*" I decided the discomfort was not too high a price to pay for a grownup hair style.

For the rest of my hair, the second procedure consisted of the traditional ritual of using twelve long, two-inch, strips of cloth. Nanita would comb out the tangles before wrapping my hair, which was very painful. I just kept reminding myself, *"Todo para estar bonita."*

Once untangled, she would wet and part my hair into twelve sections. Now came the skilled part. Nanita would wrap a six-inch piece of a brown grocery bag at the bottom of my hair and place the cloth strips horizontally across the paper wrap. She would then roll my hair around the cloth all the way to the scalp of my hair. Finally, Nanita would tie a separate knot around my rolled hair with the ends of the strips and repeat the process until my head was covered in cloth rollers. Overall, these rollers were not too hard to sleep on, probably because of the anticipation that I would have beautiful-looking hair in the morning.

If the truth be told, I ended up with funny looking curls because I rarely slept flat against my head, as I was told. Some curls dried shooting straight up from my head and others hung sideways, like cow horns. This look definitely was not what I envisioned for myself.

A few years after this weekly beauty parlor treatment, we modernized and bought a curling iron. All we had to do was heat the iron in the glass chimney of our coal oil lamp. Sometimes the iron rod would get sooty, but what the heck, I ended up with a mop of symmetrical curls. I could now bounce my hair just like Shirley Temple, a very popular child actress who danced and sang in my favorite English speaking movies during the 1930s.

Even my sister curled her waves. What a sight we were! Nanita thought we were a little wild looking, so she took us under her wing to make us a little more presentable and plastered our too-curly heads with lots of bobby pins. As she worked on our hair she would say, "*Esto les ayuda, mis hijitas,*" assuring us that her efforts would help us.

Another beauty treatment was for my elbows. I must admit, they were pretty rough, scaly, and very dark. To treat my unsightly outdoor child look, Nanita would wrap sliced cucumbers over my elbows and tie them with strips of cloth to keep them in place. Every half hour or so, she would replace them with fresh slices.

This beauty process was a real bother because if I played any games the cucumbers would fall off my elbows. I pretty much had to stay still for long periods of time. My knees usually got the treatment, too. Nanita claimed the cucumbers would soften these two rough areas. I never noticed any improvement, but it made Nanita happy, and I was glad to be treated like an adult.

Of course, nothing went to waste in our home, so the cucumbers that were left over were placed on our eyes. It was supposed to reduce puffiness and clear our eyes, but I always thought it was to keep us quiet even longer.

On many Saturday afternoons, Nanita treated my sister and me to an oatmeal facial. Nanita would make a thick paste of oatmeal and warm water. When it was done, she would place this concoction into two small cheesecloth bags. We were then ordered to rub our faces with the gooey bags. Our faces would get covered with a thin white film that made us look like Casper the Friendly Ghost. Once the oatmeal mask dried completely on our faces and our skin was taut, we would scrub it off, washing our faces several times until Nanita would announce, "*Ya basta; ahora no están tan ahumadas.*" For her, the cleaning process was enough if we were no longer so smoky looking.

How she wanted us to be light skinned like the rest of her family, not dark skinned like our Papito. To deflect her remark about the tone of our skin, she would follow-up by saying, *"Ven que suave,"* pretending that she was solely concerned with the softness of our skin. She often let us put on the wonderful smelling rose lotion that she concocted from crushed rose petals and glycerin. I felt beautiful!

Nanita would sometimes look at us with calculating eyes and mutter, *"Que cabello tan josco."* Luckily, the treatment for dingy hair would wait until evening, when we washed and rinsed our hair with vinegar to make it shiny.

The only task left was putting calcimine lotion on our legs. This treatment was supposed to bleach them, but I never saw any difference. We kept the lotion on until it dried, and then washed it off. I guess we were supposed to look like the white-washed walls, but our legs remained dark. Poor Nanita. She tried so hard and we tried to cooperate, but the Good Lord blessed us with the exceptional good looks of our beautiful brown-skinned Papito.

When she wasn't too tired, Nanita gave us a *frotada*. She claimed the mini-massage would improve our circulation and make us pretty. In return, we would give Nanita a *frotada*, but she would quickly say she had to get some work done and leave us. I think we were doing it wrong. What we could count on from Nanita or Mamita was a daily *frotada* of the scalp. They would run their fingers through our hair to get the circulation going.

Laxatives were a key topic of conversation during our beauty sessions. Nanita would say, *"Cuando tus interiores están limpios, se enseñan en tus pieles."* I never saw a connection between clean insides and the quality of my skin, but maybe it was because I hated the laxatives and didn't want to admit they might help. I was sure that one didn't need to sit in the outhouse all day in order to look beautiful.

One beauty ritual that Nanita did not approve of was the use of makeup. In fact, we weren't allowed to wear any whatsoever. Nanita would remind us that, *"No mas las mujeres de la calle usan maquillaje."* Even though Nanita had told us that only women of the night wear makeup, Vera and I did try rubbing rose petals on our lips and cheeks when she was not around. We were sure it enhanced our beauty. Besides, I never had the courage to ask who these women were. I wondered, "Did we know some?" "Were they our friends?"

When I was older, it bothered me when I saw high school girls wearing lipstick. I wanted to look like them and not feel different. I asked myself, Why couldn't I join in the fun? They surely were not women of the night. While not wearing lipstick hurt my pride just a little, I was confident knowing other beauty secrets that they did not.

I'll never forget Nanita saying, *"Ahora si parecen como la gente, mis hijitas."* When she affirmed that her granddaughters were presentable, I understood that I was fortified by Nanita's many beauty traditions. To me, this was a game of how to fool Mother Nature.

Chapter 18: Dances in the Schoolhouse

Dancing was my great joy.

For me, getting ready for, going to, and returning from a dance was half the fun of actually being at the dance. Getting ready required all the good-natured commotion of catching the horses, harnessing them, and hitching them to the wagon. Once our transportation was ready, we would all pile in for the family ride to wherever the *fiesta* was held. It could be in the schoolhouse, which was not too far from the *ranchito*, or it could be at the dance hall in Sapelló.

Preparation for the trip was Rampo's job, and we helped all we could. We'd load the wagon box with the mattress, the patch-work quilts, and the many multi-colored pillows. Rampo worried we'd fall when jumping on and off the wagon and would constantly warn us to be careful, repeating, *"Cuidado."*

Nanita's job, after making sure we looked presentable, was to pack the treats. We could count on goodies like *tortilla* wedges with *jalea de capulín* – choke cherry jelly. Other times, she fried *sopaipillas* that were so puffed up they looked as though they were going to burst. On occasion, she even included some store-bought candy. Nanita also filled the ever-present big glass jars with water, which would quench our thirst for the several hours we'd be away from home.

Nanita would mumble, *"Espero que tengamos suficiente comida para el largo tiempo en que estaremos afuera de la casa. Los niños siempre tienen hambre."* She was worried about whether she had packed enough food to keep us kids happy for such a long time away from home.

Once we got on the way, Nanita would begin praying. Later she invited us kids to sing along with her, which we did at the top of our lungs. Sometimes she told us stories, but mostly she pointed out what we were seeing along the road and out into the far distance. There was so much to see and talk about. It was a beautiful countryside.

I especially loved the dances at the schoolhouse. They were so vibrant! The school was a small one-room building with a wooden door at the front and two small paned windows on opposite sides of the walls. At the back of the room was a large blackboard. The floors were made of rough lumber, hammered on a wooden frame. The floors were scrubbed often to settle the dust caused by muddy shoes. The adobe walls were white and made from the bleached dirt that was found in several hills in the immediate area. The only real problem was that if you leaned on the wall your clothes got a chalky powder on them and it could not easily be brushed off. Consequently, lots of white backs were seen dancing the night away.

When there was going to be a dance, all the desks, including the teacher's, were pushed against the walls. Doing so opened a large space where we could dance to our hearts' content. The volunteer musicians set up their instruments in front of the blackboard. They could see who was dancing and who was coming and going. None of the musicians ever practiced together as a group. They just played whatever song they agreed upon right there at the dance. Usually, but not necessarily, the leader was the one who played the best. The instruments were mostly limited to guitars and violins. Sometimes an accordion player showed up. Almost everyone in attendance knew the words of all the songs that they played, so everyone sang as they danced. We were a happy, joyous group.

Nanita and Rampo often were the first couple on the floor, with Junior and I following. Vera already was old enough to get asked to dance, so we would watch her dancing with some handsome young man. Rampo also asked Mamita to dance, but sometimes friends of the family would invite her to dance. She did not seem to have as much fun at the dance as Nanita.

Many couples danced, but groups of young children, children with their mothers, and women danced together without male partners. Any dance step was accepted, and the aim of the evening was simply to have fun. We danced polkas, the quick-stepped *shotis* with lots of twirling, waltzes, the romantic *boleros*, and anything else our musicians knew how to play. Some of these special dances required one to learn simple steps, and others intricate steps. Sometimes, people stood by to watch a few of the grownups who were skilled dancers.

An entertaining dance was *el Baile del Paño*, the Handkerchief Dance. As couples were dancing, the *bastonero* or dance director would hand a handkerchief to one duo. Everyone would continue dancing until the music suddenly stopped and the couple would then hand the handkerchief to another couple. The two who passed the handkerchief would then have to leave the dance floor. The last couple handed the handkerchief was announced the winner. They danced a set alone to the loud clapping and singing of the entire gathering.

The broom dance, *el Baile de la Escoba*, was a very similar dance to the *Baile del Paño* and just as much fun. As couples danced, a person would hand one of the partners a broom. The other partner would have to sit down. The one with the broom would dance around until he decided the next person that would get the broom. The dance continued until only one person was left dancing with the broom amongst wild cheering and thunderous clapping.

La Varsoviana also was a favorite, but only danced once or twice during the night. This slow, genteel type of dance in three-quarter time originated in Poland. It combined the waltz, the mazurka, and the polka. That dance later became well known in English speaking gatherings as "Put Your Little Foot." I learned as an adult that Conrad Hilton, the New Mexican millionaire, requested this special dance at every large social function he attended, the world over. Little did we know in Sapelló that it was such a famous dance. We also danced *la Raspa*, which was a faster version of the "Mexican Hat Dance."

An annual dance celebrated on Easter was *el Baile de los Cascarones*, the "Dance of the Confetti-Filled Eggshells." During the dark months of Lent, all the valley families decorated hollowed out chicken eggs and filled them with confetti, then sealed the small hole where they were filled with a thin piece of paper. At our gatherings, we broke them on each other's heads as we were dancing. The breaking of the eggs usually was done from behind, so the dancer did not expect it. Sometimes the egg was either thrown or crushed, whichever way you best could get to your intended. Now that was a *fiesta*!

El Baile del Amarre took place toward the end of our social gatherings. A *lazo* made of a long, silk scarf was placed on the shoulders of the person who stood out, for whatever logical or silly reason, and this indicated that they were selected to sponsor the next dance, which meant selecting the place, time, and musicians. You were *amarrado* or *amarrada*, bound and selected, to plan the logistics for the next dance. The sponsor also was responsible for finding volunteers to help clean the schoolhouse or dance hall before and after the dance. Finding help was never a problem; the musicians or other late revelers always were around to volunteer.

The fun part of this dance was the selection of the sponsor. This person or couple might be selected for their unique attire or for some first-time action or accomplishment. The list of possibilities was endless. Maybe it was a person dancing with their child for the first time; or a woman who was wearing a red dress or a ribbon in her hair; or a man who was wearing new shoes or who had a fresh haircut; or a man who danced with a woman he had never danced with before.

Just before the dance would end, there would be much discussion with the "honored" sponsor about the date for the next dance and where it would be held. Once decided, the musicians would stop playing and everyone would stand and listen to the *amarrado* or *amarrada* announce the next date and place for a dance. Most dances were held about every two weeks, about as long as everyone wanted to wait. Every child and adult loved to dance. Dancing defined who we were.

Occasionally at our dances, a few men would start a fist fight, often over a girl. Young men were the usual trouble makers, but they were not allowed to disrupt the dance for too long. As soon as a fight started, the dance stopped, and the women would quickly round up the children and herd them towards the musicians at the back of the room. At the same time, the older men would rush to break up the fight. If the men that were fighting did not stop immediately, they were led outside and allowed to pound on each other for a while longer. Meanwhile, the women waited inside and gossiped about why the young men were fighting. They also managed to comb our hair, straighten out our bows and ties, and make us children presentable for the next set of dances. A mother's job was never done, even at a dance.

After a few minutes, the older men would stop the fight, so the dancing could continue. The fighters returned a short time later with a few of the older gentlemen who had remained outside with them. They were cleaned up and looked sheepish. I never saw the same two young men ever fight again. I guess the sermon they got while outside was sobering.

Oh! The fighting was not limited to the men. One time, a couple of women got into it. It was the only fight between women that I ever saw, but the gossip was that there had been others. Nanita never let us forget how terrible it looked for women to fight. The women who were fighting grabbed each other's hair and pulled at each other. They also clawed their faces with their nails. The lighter side of the squabble was what they were saying to each other. I had never heard anything like it. One shouted that the other was missing a front tooth and called her *molacha*. She added that she needed to get some new teeth. The other retorted, that she should get some teeth for her. At that remark, the first woman countered that she would get dog teeth for her big mouth. At this point, the husbands and friends moved the two off the dance floor and carried them outside still screaming and kicking.

While the fight happened quickly, we were shocked that women actually brawled. This fight was very different from the men's fights we had seen and very different in another way too. Those women, their husbands, and their families did not show up for months at the dances. When they finally returned, they mingled right in as if nothing had happened and it did not seem to bother anyone. I don't recall anyone referring to the fight. I came to believe that good dance parties made people forget a lot of things.

One event on our way home stands out vividly in my mind. We had stayed late after a dance, and did not return until after sundown. It was a beautiful, still night and the land was well-lit from the full moon and thousands of twinkling stars. We were discussing the beauty of the sky and making up stories about what we were seeing when Rampo told us to be very quiet. He pointed in front of the horses. There, as though the road belonged to them, strolled a mama skunk and her two little black and white babies. Rampo slowed the horses down to a mere walk and whispered, "*No debemos asustarlos, o la mamá puede rociarnos.*" We knew from experience that we must not scare them, or the mama might squirt us.

We must have followed them at a snail's pace for perhaps fifteen minutes, all of us quiet with only an occasional whisper to point something out. Finally, the skunks veered off the road and we were able to pick up speed to continue our journey home and laugh about the experience. Rampo encouraged the horses to go faster with both his voice and the reins. In no time we were home. With all the excitement, we were too tired to help Rampo unhitch the horses.

We went straight to bed. I dreamed all night of dancing and could hear the music playing my favorite songs. For the rest of my life I never turned down a single dance.

LESSONS

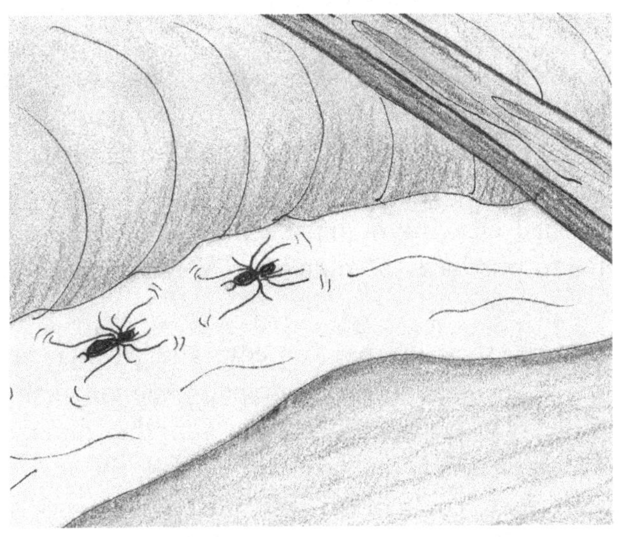

Chapter 19: Las Acequias

Las acequias are the best playgrounds for an inquisitive mind.

But my playground came with a history and rules. Rampo explained that if ranchers high in the mountain hoarded the water for their fields, those downriver suffered. Along Las Manuelitas Creek people regulated the use of water through *las acequias*. Rampo told us that these irrigation practices were used in Egypt, Spain, and by indigenous tribes across the Americas for hundreds of years. When the early Spaniards settled in northern New Mexico, they applied the same ancient tradition of community-based *acequias*.

Las acequias are so treasured that this water ethic has been passed down over hundreds of years through an *Acequia* Association to *parciantes*, individual owners or irrigators, who own water rights along *la acequia*. *Los parciantes* in turn pledge to maintain a healthy and secure source of water on their portion of *la acequia*.

Each spring, the members elect a *mayordomo* or ditch boss and a commission to oversee the release of water, assess how much water each member can use to flood-irrigate their land based on the size of their property, and determine when *las acequias* need cleaning or repair. The *parciantes* also pay a small fee to purchase the parts needed for the main cutoff valves.

Paying an association fee also covers help when needed. Sometimes repairs are needed to repair *presas* or small dams used to divert water from a creek to a mother ditch, called *la acequia madre*. When repairs are needed, the *mayordomo* asks *parciantes* to come on an appointed day to work. If one cannot go, he has to send an able-bodied man in his place. If he does not, he is assessed a daily charge.

So much care is needed to maintain *las acequias*. The turnout drainage easement or *desagüe* on each farm also requires attention. It is there that the water can be diverted back into the creek or forwarded to the property of a *vecino*. If a bank breaks, water can flood a home, an orchard, or an entire field.

Wooden troughs known as *canoas* are another key *acequia* element that frequently has to be fixed. They are designed to carry water across a property from one high place to another without wasting water, but are rather flimsy. We were cautioned not to go in them. We only did so a few times when we were in a great hurry to get to where we wanted to play.

One of the last major pieces of the *acequia* is *la compuerta*, a heavy lumber head gate located on each *parciante's* farm. The head gate can be raised for water to flow from *la acequia* down toward the owner's *milpas* or cornfields and *huertas* or vegetable gardens. When the ditches are all cleaned and repaired in late March and early April, a little water is released to see if there are any problems. If the water flows with no leaks, *la compuerta* is lifted for the water to run into the fields.

Las acequias are usually the fullest in May because that is when the creek floods. That is right before the fields are planted and there is typically enough water for the farmers' needs. The only problem they incur during this season is damage from *las nutrias*. Beavers like to cut and topple trees, usually over *el desagüe*, which then causes the water to spill out everywhere. The *parciantes* also have to remove clogging that results from dry leaves, tree roots, and other kinds of debris. That is hard work and I remember everyone getting into the act, even the children. We would hold the banks in place with our hands while the adults would put shovels full of dry dirt around the mud we tried to hold. As we worked, the killdeer birds ran around near us on their tiny, skinny legs and made their funny shrill birdcalls. I have to admit that I would rather have been chasing the birds than working.

If water was released into an alfalfa field, but then disappeared and reappeared in another field, we knew we had another kind of problem: *Perritos del agua.* In northern New Mexico, we disliked these prairie dogs that made tunnels because of the flooding they caused.

Rampo would have us quickly close up the holes with stones and sticks and anything else handy, while he filled them with huge shovels full of dirt. Those gaping holes would eat everything up, and at times it seemed like we never would be able to stop the water from escaping. Hours later and with much effort, we sometimes were able to seal the holes. If we took too long, Rampo would lose his allotted time and could no longer use the ditch water. He would have to close his *compuerta* and let the water run to the next user. That is when the *perritos* won that round of watering.

It is not until late autumn that the *mayordomo's* job and the farmers' work is finished. By then, there is no more water in the creek to divert to the ditches, and the cool fall air ends the growing cycle. Another season has gone by and the knowledge learned is put to rest until the following spring.

All children were advised to be very careful around *las acequias*, but we were also taught to love them for the gift of life they provided us. During our free time, we kids loved the endless fun of playing beside the cool and verdant *acequias*. Along the tall banks grew plants, bushes, and even trees. Between the larger plants, the ground was covered with thatches of green grass interspersed with lots of flowers of every color.

Every so often, a board was laid across the ditch to serve as a footbridge. We used the planks to sit and hang our feet into the cool moving water. Sometimes we used the plank to climb down and get into the water. Of course, we carefully left our shoes and socks on *el banco de la acequia*. Even sitting on the bank of the ditch, we didn't dare get dirty. If we did, it would reveal to Mamita or our *abuelos* where we had been.

A neighbor child often played a game with the *cabrillas* that scurried around on the surface of the water. He would catch a water spider and hold it between his thumb and forefinger just below the first set of the spider's little eight legs. In unison, we would ask the *cabrilla*, "*¿Dónde está Díos?*" Immediately, the two front legs would point skyward to God. We'd then ask, "*¿Dònde está el Diablo?*" Sure enough, the little legs would point downward to the Devil. We would ask the questions over and over as we ran around the boy holding the spider. The strange thing was that the game worked only when that neighbor child held the *cabrilla*; I wonder what he was pulling, besides our legs.

Chapter 20: Our Own Healer

I yelled, "*¡Junior, mira quien viene!*

Looking down the dirt road, I could see a distant figure walking towards the house and kicking up an unusual amount of dust. "*Tal vez, Nanita nos diga que no tenemos que sacar yerbas mientras que visitan.*" I was hopeful that a visitor would mean a break from weeding.

As we continued to watch the stranger, we noticed that he walked quickly, rather than the usual leisurely fashion of our *compadres* and *comadres*. Junior mumbled to himself, "*No parece que viene no más a visitar. Te apuesto que alguien está enfermo.*" He was sure that such a quick pace meant that someone was ill.

Junior always surprised me when he spoke with adult wisdom. While holding a fist full of the offensive weeds, I suggested hopefully that we slow down just in case we could stop working.

We continued watching and lazily pulled weeds as the stranger progressed up the road. Getting bored, we began laughing at the funny spots of dirt on each other's faces and promptly forgot there might be some urgency in our guest's visit. Before we knew it, the visitor, who turned out to be one of our grandparents' *compadres*, finally reached the front yard. Nanita magically appeared at her front door and invited the neighbor in out of the sun.

"*¡Buenos días! ¿Cómo está la familia?*" she greeted her *compadre* and asked after his family. Then she asked him to take a seat in the living room.

Out of breath, the *compadre* stayed standing and quickly said, "*Lo siento, Doña Juanita, no puedo visitar. Mi esposa está muy enferma y me envió a buscarte.*"

At the news that he was not there for a visit, but on behalf of his sick wife, Nanita asked with a concerned voice, "*¿Qué pasa con tu esposa?*" Instead of waiting to find out what was wrong with his wife, she instantly took off her apron and headed into the kitchen to start gathering her herbs.

He replied, relaxing a little after seeing she was preparing to come right away, "*Su estómago. Ha tenido dolor toda la noche. Y yo no puedo hacer nada por ella. Se necesita tu ayuda.*" The stomach pains that she had suffered all night had led her husband to seek Nanita's help.

Nanita paused long enough in her preparations to come to the door where we were peeking in and called us inside. We smiled our "all-knowing" smiles to each other, happy that we were really going to get a reprieve from pulling weeds. Someone else's great discomfort usually meant great fun for us, because, while Nanita did the doctoring, we got to play with the neighbor's kids at their house instead of ours.

We were used to these sudden changes in our daily routine because feeding families was not the only thing Nanita did to help her many *compadres* and *comadres*. Nanita helped take care of the sick and the injured throughout the entire valley. With herbs and many prayers, she did everything that possibly could be done regarding healing.

There were no doctors nearby, and if there had been, the people did not have enough money to pay for their treatment. Nanita's visits were free and no one was afraid of her no matter what she did to help them. When Nanita was helping someone who was quite ill, she constantly muttered to herself that she hoped God would hear her and help her choose the right plant to make the proper salve or tea. Although Nanita claimed she was not a *curandera*, a traditional folk healer or herb doctor, she did not hesitate to apply the treatments learned from her mother and from her own successful experiments.

I never understood why Nanita's patients never whimpered, even though they were very ill and in pain. Maybe they did not want to scare away their only doctor, my Nanita. When we returned home and after supper, she had us kneel at her altarcito. An integral part of Nanita's healing practice was the rosary and special prayers called *novenas*. She would have us add extra novenas to help her patients get well. She always called upon God to help intervene in healing the sick.

Nanita helped pregnant women too, but I don't recall that she ever delivered a baby. For that job, there were *parteras*. These midwives were brought from other communities a couple of days before the blessed event. Often Nanita stayed at the home of the woman giving birth on the day of the birth, taking care of the entire family. My *abuelos* also were involved in the new birth in another way. They were asked to be baptismal sponsors of at least one godchild in almost every family in their community. They counted fifty-nine of these *haijados* that they sponsored.

In the spring and summer, Nanita would take us to collect various herbs and roots for anticipated illnesses. These outings turned into all-day affairs, and a good excuse to have a picnic. On those sunny days, we took water in large jars along with *tortillas* filled with something delicious from Nanita's kitchen. She always found a beautiful place to sit and eat.

Depending on what plants we were to gather, Nanita would take us into the woods, along the creek bank, or into the fields early in the morning. She would caution us against sunstroke as we went out, saying: *"Salimos temprano cuando todavía no hace tanto calor, porque nos podemos dar una asoleada."*

While this was before the days of knowing the relationship between skin cancer and UV rays, she only allowed us to expose ourselves to the sun for short periods of time. Probably, Nanita kept our tanning short because she hated for her two granddaughters to get too dark-skinned since she and Mamita were so fair-skinned. They seemed not to worry about my brother because he was fair skinned like them and they knew he would not get *prieto* like his sisters. However, Nanita would tell us we all needed a little sun. She appeared to know something no one else in our family seemed to know, and that was the power of the sun and its health benefits.

In the afternoon, we would trudge back to the house with gunnysacks over our backs filled with a variety of roots and plants. Nanita would later set the plants out to dry by putting the small plants in paper bags and hanging the larger plants in the tack room. Sometimes she would immediately share her plants with the neighbors and her *comadres*. I think she thought that in this manner she could relinquish at least a small portion of her medical duties; however, no one seemed inclined to take on this responsibility. Everyone that was sick only wanted to see Doña Juanita. With her around, no one seemed to feel that they needed to learn the skills that she had acquired over the years.

For curing sores, Nanita did not have to rely on her many herbs and plants. She would just take a yellow bar of her soap, home-made with lye, lard and a few ashes. She would then mix it with a little bit of water and sugar, and mash it into a paste. This mixture was then placed on a boil or sometimes on an open sore to draw out the infection. After much pressing around the sore spot, Nanita would get the pus to come out. Her last step was to bandage the wound with cheesecloth. Most patients felt better instantly. Another treatment Nanita used for a wound with pus was applying *trementina*, or pitch, from evergreen trees. She chewed it and placed it on the wound before bandaging it.

When Vera had a badly infected hangnail, Nanita soaked a red *chile* pod in warm water until it was soft and pliable. Then she laid it on the sore, wrapped it with a white cloth, and kept it covered for several days. Poor Vera, her finger hurt terribly, but after the treatment she got better, and never pulled on her nails again.

Some people in the community believed that sores were contagious and needed to be medicated quickly. Many believed that certain persons could *inconar,* making another person's sore spot get even worse. Even worse, most people never knew who the carrier might be. Nanita knew some of the carriers by name and said that we had to be very careful if we were ill and one of them was around. If one of those persons visited, we were made to stay in another room until the person left. Nanita was not taking chances with her most prized possessions, her grandchildren.

Of course, Nanita treated everyone for insect bites. I am allergic to the darn stings, so I was Nanita's frequent client. She would use the rich black mud that we brought from the creek for that medication; ditch mud or reddish looking mud had no healing powers. Nanita would place the thick black mud on the bite, rub it a little bit and then cover it with a piece of cloth. The cold mud felt good and it kept us from scratching for long periods of time. We all seemed to feel better with the mudpacks. I guess the mud dissolved the stingers and poison.

Adding to her other skills, Nanita learned how to give rubdowns or *frotadas.* She was good at taking care of back pains and sore arms and legs using only *Aceite del Volcán* and *Aceite de la Virgen de Guadalupe*, volcano oil and Virgin of Guadalupe oil. Nanita swore by the power of those two oils. She also made sure that, along with the massages, her clients drank different kinds of teas, but mostly peppermint. With a name like *yerba buena*, peppermint was bound to always do some good.

Rubbing the stomach was used for treating *susto*, a panic attack. Nanita would have you lay on her bed as she massaged your stomach that she said was *elevada* under the ribs due to the scare. As she massaged your stomach, it would relax and go back to its normal position. It definitely made you feel better. Of course, several hot teas went with the massage and usually one fell asleep during, or right after, this procedure.

For stomach aches, cramps, and most colds, the medication was very similar. Nanita had us drink lots of very hot teas made from *poleo* – penny royal, *yerba buena* – peppermint, *romerillo* – silver sage, and *estafiate* – black sage, among many others. We also drank plenty of *altamisa* – mugwort. While drinking the teas, we had to stay in bed wrapped in blankets and perspire until our illness went away. The wetter we got, the sooner we recovered from our ailment. We never were left alone during these treatments. Some member of the family always stayed close to take care of us and keep us covered, even if it was in the middle of June. It was worth getting a cold; so much attention and love was showered on us.

Up and down the valleys, everyone believed that *oshá*, or yucca root, kept the evil spirits away. It was a powerful medicine used like a charm. An evil person or a witch would not come close to a person who had *oshá* on their body. It was considered so powerful that it kept the rattlesnakes away too. Rampo always had a piece of *oshá* in the top pocket of his bib overalls, and Nanita always checked to make sure it was there before he went outside in the morning. It was at exactly the same time that she reminded him to check for his clean handkerchief and the bandana he was supposed to put on his neck when the sun got hot.

It was smart not to cough when Nanita was around because she would immediately give you some awful tasting stuff to make it go away. The one she swore by was a teaspoon of lamp coal oil mixed with a little sugar. We were to keep it in our mouths for as long as possible. The sugar was good, but the oil was terrible. If that medicine didn't stop our cough, we got the Vicks treatment. She would rub Vicks all over our chests, and then put pieces of flannel cloth on the pot-bellied stove and, when hot, place immediately on us. More than once, we screamed bloody murder that she was burning us. Our chests would be red because the cloths were so hot. For some reason, we would go to sleep and always felt better upon waking. Over all, we might be considered very lucky. The neighbor children insisted they had to drink the hot water from boiled goat *carajones* – droppings. At least we were spared that experience.

For a severe *calentura* or *fiebre*, there was nothing like *papas con vinagre.* The potatoes with vinegar were placed on your forehead and on the bottom of your feet. They were held in place with a cloth band. This treatment brought the fever down so quickly, you didn't know what happened. As the fever left, the *papas* would get hot and turn brown. Nanita would replace the hot *papas* with fresh ones over and over until the fever was gone. What a French fry machine we turned out to be! But the truth is that many a time we got rid of our fevers with this simple remedy.

One of Nanita's favorite ways to treat headaches was with the stamps from the little sacks of tobacco. She would place the stamps over our temples and hold them down with her fingers until they stuck to our skin. In our teen years, we regularly teased Nanita by asking her where the person with the stamps on the forehead was going to be shipped. She did not find this joke amusing. Years later, I learned that applying pressure to certain points of your body was indeed very helpful to remove pain. Smart Nanita!

Oh, but there was another unwelcome remedy that was a constant in our lives. Every Saturday whether we needed it or not, we had to take a *purgante* before our bath. Vera, Junior, and I disliked these laxatives with a passion. A tablespoon of any of her remedies was enough to loosen your bowels. Oh God, were we ever squeaky clean!

One week we got castor oil and another time it was Epsom salts. Awful. Ugh! And yes, we had our share of enemas. A pink rubber bag full of warm water with a little soap was hung up high over the bed and we got the treatment. Enemas usually were reserved for serious stomach aches or high fevers.

This treatment was not exactly for illnesses, but we all knew about *la mala suerte* and *el mal ojo*. Both bad luck and the evil eye required special *remedios.* To keep away *la mala suerte*, you carried a remedy such as a piece of *osha* in your pocket, wore a scapular medal around your neck, and of course, kept a rosary in your pocket or purse.

For *el mal ojo*, the *remedio* was slightly more complicated. Luckily for me, I never had a problem with the evil eye. It seemed to be reserved for cute children. You were not supposed to admire a pretty baby too much because you could give the child the *mal ojo* and make the child sick with headaches, fever, and certainly lots of vomiting.

When a baby was admired too much, Nanita forced the parents to take the necessary precautions. They had to take a gulp of water in their mouth and transfer that water from their mouth into the mouth of their baby. If there was a person named Manuel or Manuela nearby, they were asked to give the water to the child. Children never seemed to die from the *mal ojo*, so maybe the remedy worked. If a child got sick afterwards, Nanita used *alucema*. This lavender was the same *remedio* to treat a colicky baby.

Over several summers, I was a mess with what everyone said was a severe case of poison ivy. My body was covered with tiny blisters and my eyes were swollen shut. Nanita would make a small tent in the middle of the living room by placing two high backed chairs back to back and cover them entirely with a white sheet while I sat inside the enclosure. This "mini-tent" gave me privacy because I was so raw that I could not wear clothes. She reduced the pain by smearing me with every ointment she could think of. What I thought helped stop the itch the most was a rub down with baking soda or starch after taking a cool bath. Those two things soothed my skin and helped me to sleep without scratching, at least until I started itching again.

The idea of the tent also was to keep me from being lonely. Other children played around the tent and although we could not see each other, it was a comfort to hear them near me. The last summer I broke out with the blisters, it was so severe that they had to call a doctor. He diagnosed it as poison oak, not poison ivy! The doctor gave me some pills to take internally and a special ointment for my blisters. I was cured in a few days and never had another poison oak breakout. Nanita put on her detective cap and went walking to all the places I had played until she figured out how I had gotten poison oak. She determined that I was holding on to the poison oak branches while trying to avoid falling into the poison ivy plants along the creek edges.

Our *vecinos* and our family were lucky to have Nanita. I was lucky to have my Nanita. If she did not know what to do when someone was sick, she invented a treatment. If there was a problem, she investigated. She took responsibility and initiative when no one else would.

Chapter 21: Cleansing Rituals

If a prize had been awarded for the cleanest family of the year, we surely would have won.

As she did with our personal cleansing rituals to prepare for church, Nanita paid attention to detail in cleaning her house. To her, cleanliness was considered a virtue right next to Godliness, and she never let us forget it.

When it looked like we would have a warm spell, Nanita would tell Rampo she wanted to wash the next day. That was all she said, and Rampo would immediately tell us, "*Vamos a partir leña.*" It was time to chop wood.

We would jump up and leave whatever we were doing and go with him to the giant woodpile. Before splitting the wood, Rampo would make sure his two axes were very sharp. His round twelve-inch wide whetstone had a hole in the middle and looked much like a doughnut. One of us would crank the disk, mounted on a simple wooden frame with clamps, and make it turn as fast as we could. Meanwhile,

Rampo would place his axe, or sometimes his saw, right on the turning whetstone to sharpen the edges. The stone would get hot, so we would pour cold water over it to cool it down.

If we needed to cut some *trozos*, he would make sure his saw was extra sharp. It was a long saw with handles on each end. I loved to be at one end and saw away at the thick logs. I associated it with a teeter-totter. I liked to say, "Your turn, my turn, your turn, my turn." And that saw would make a whiny singsong. Sometimes it would get hot, and we had to wait a few minutes for it to cool down. We made a game of everything.

Rampo often let us try to split the wood. He showed us the correct way to swing the axe, where to stand, how to lean the wood against another piece, and how much force to exert. He would demonstrate and make it seem so easy. Then we would beg him to let us try. Even though we followed his directions exactly, we seldom split the logs unless he started the cut for us. We would tell Rampo, *"Está muy dura la leña."* He would smile at us as we continued with our feeble attempts to cut the hard wood.

Once chopped, we took the wood to the area Nanita used for washing clothes, and stacked the wood close to the tub, but not too close to the house. After all, we didn't want the flying embers to catch the house on fire. We made dozens of trips back and forth because we could only carry two or three sticks of wood at a time. It was the running that was fun, and also the competition to see who could run the fastest and bring the most wood.

When Rampo decided we had brought enough wood, we moved on to the next chore. We now had to rake the *palitos* and pieces of *ocote*, and put them in buckets, pans, or boxes. We carried the lighter wood chips and pitch wood to the tub, and Rampo took care of the heavier ones. He always carefully arranged the *palitos* around the bottom of the tub and added sticks of wood on top of them. Rampo would then explain how we needed to leave space for the air to get in and help the fire burn quickly. But the most important thing was that the *ocote* be placed strategically in various places to get a good fire going. After our wood chopping, stacking, and positioning chores were done, we raked the whole area to make it look nice and clean just the way Nanita liked it.

We now had one last job and that was to fill the tubs with water. If the ditch had water, it did not take long to fill them up. If we had to go to the well, the walk was much farther. In either case, it was tiring work because we had to fill two ten-pound lard cans each with that precious water. It took lots of trips to fill our containers. Fortunately, Rampo and Nanita joined the water brigade using larger buckets.

Once the tubs were full, Nanita would announce that we could quit working for the evening. *"Vamos a ver si hay algo bueno para comer."* When she said that there might be something good to eat, we knew then that we would be rewarded with one of Nanita's sweet treats.

Early the next morning, we would find the kindling and wood burning under one of the tubs. I never knew who lit it, but both Rampo and Nanita kept the fire going for a very long time until the wash water was hot. Nanita then took over and we never saw Rampo anywhere near the wash again.

Junior and I stayed to help Nanita move the buckets of hot water from the big tub to the tub with a washer board. Now the washing began. Nanita's hands would get rough and red from the boiling water and the harsh bar of lye soap. The rest of us would help scrub too. Up and down the washboard, stopping occasionally to add more soap. Sometimes we used a brush on difficult spots, like the collars of the work shirts.

We chanted silently to ourselves, *"Limpienlas bien,"* so that we would clean them well.

After the clothes were scrubbed, we wrung them out as much as we could, and then threw them into the tub that held cold rinse water. We swirled them around and wrung them out before putting them in empty buckets and pans to later hang on the clothesline. We placed all the white items in the pans with water and a bluing agent; that way our clothes would be snowy white. Sometimes we laid the small white articles on top of bushes if there wasn't a strong wind. Nanita thought the clothes that got direct sun got whiter than those hanging on the clotheslines.

She also had us put the shirts, aprons, tablecloths, and the crocheted edges of the top sheets and pillow cases into the pans filled with starch. Once they were well coated with starch, we could then put them on the clothes lines or bushes.

The washing took many hours of hard labor, but there still was more to be done. Nanita did not want to waste the soapy or rinse waters. So, we had to water all the flowerbeds with it. The soap killed many bugs and our flowers would be even prettier. Even they got washed with soap and water. Wow, what cleanliness!

All day long, we checked the clothes for the right degree of dryness. The items that were not going to be ironed, like underwear, were left to completely dry. The rest of the clothes were taken indoors slightly damp, so we could then iron them if there was still enough daylight. If not, the ironing was left until the following day. Heating the iron on the stove was the last thing we did. The kitchen got very hot, so usually the ironing was done on the big porch. We were exhausted by the end of the day, but Nanita made sure we were well fed, hugged, and, of course, cleaned before we said our prayers and collapsed into a deep sleep.

One chore I was glad to do only once a year was washing the hand-made wool mattresses and pillows. Every summer we would take the wool out of the bedding and thoroughly wash it. We were told it was another cleaning tradition in our family, but over the years I learned that this annual chore allowed the wool to breath better and clean the residual dust from our bodies.

Washing the wool was similar to washing clothes. We washed each piece of wool by hand in a tub with soapy water and then rinsed it, piece-by-piece, in another tub filled with clean water. The mattress cover was washed separately using a laundry washboard and a stiff brush. After rinsing out the suds, we faced the challenge of squeezing the water out of the material. We only had our hands to do this job, so all of us had to take turns squeezing out as much of the water as we could. Once that work was done, it took the entire family to get the mattress cover on the clothesline; some of us had the job of keeping it off the ground. Others struggled to hold the heavy, wet mattress cover on the clothesline and clamp it with the wooden clothespins.

After all the washing was done, we would return to the cleaned wool and carefully spread the pieces out on large canvas sheets to dry in the sun. We always prayed that it would not get cloudy or rain. Most times it would take more than two days for the cover and the wool to dry. To speed the drying along, we had to keep flipping the wool so that the damp side was up toward the sun. We could do little with the huge cover on the line. It just had to dry in its own time.

When all the bedding was dried, another day or so of hard work remained to be done. We had to stuff the clean wool back inside the covers. We would stuff small sections at a time and then tie it down with two inner straps that were sewn into the mattress cover. It was hard to get into those areas, so us skinny kids would crawl way inside of the cover to do the work. The mattress cover was stuffed outside in the middle of the *patio* with the sun beating on us. It was stifling hot and suffocating inside the mattress for any length of time, so everyone had to work fast.

But there's more. With all these chores done, we still faced the daily cleaning of the house. Needless to say, Nanita's and our house in Las Vegas was spotless with well-scrubbed wooden floors and shiny windowpanes. Everything was always super clean and in its place. At the *ranchito*, Nanita made sure that the dirt patio also was swept clean. If the *patio* was not swept exceptionally well, Mamita and Nanita would remind us that the witches would come at night to dance on the dirt and cast their spells. We kids couldn't let that happen.

Yes! By the end of each day at the *ranchito*, we were exhausted, but we never complained. Time flew by quickly being engaged in the company of our loving family. We learned so many lessons, including the tradition of staying clean.

Chapter 22: Scary Stories and Dichos

Something scratched on the window from the outside.

Dark shadows grew in the corners of the house. In the evening or at night, when we misbehaved, we learned that evil spirits lurked everywhere, waiting to take away bad children. At that age, we believed whatever Rampo and Nanita told us and we were very afraid. Many nights, we would keep our eyes closed tight from fear.

A spooky story they would tell us was about *El Coco*. We did not ask how *El Coco* came to be or what he looked like exactly. We just knew he was a ghost-like monster, and we were just plain scared of him. All we had to be told is that he would take ill-behaved kids away to never be heard from again. We didn't need to see him to believe it.

The story of *La Llorona*, the Crying Woman, also put fear in us. Many versions of *La Llorona* exist, but we were told that a woman who had to give up her children could be heard wailing in search of her lost babies along the *acequias* throughout the night. If she found you in the *acequias, La Llorona* would take you to become her child. With ditches all around, it was easy to believe what they told us. Every noise we heard, we knew it was *La Llorona.* The howling winds at the base of the mountain only fueled our fears.

We also were led to believe that the hoot of an owl was a bad omen. When we were in bed we would cover up to our ears with blankets and pillows, to block out the sound of the owl. Still we would hear the owls because our house was at the base of the mountain with hundreds of evergreens, which were home to birds of prey galore. It made for many chilling nights.

Of course, if we fought with each other, we could get into serious trouble. Nanita always told us that if we raised our hand to strike a sibling, our hand would turn to wood, becoming a *mano de palo.* If we were about to strike, the one who was going to receive the blow would yell, *"Se te va a secar la mano."* Fear of a hand drying up usually stopped the fight immediately.

All in all, the scary stories did reinforce the manners our *abuelos* wanted to instill in us children, or rather it helped us to avoid the bad behavior. Many Hispanics in New Mexico pass these legends from generation to generation. My *abuelos* were not alone in applying these legendary pranks on their children. Their stories later became useful tools for expressing the obvious and breaking the ice with friends and colleagues who heard similar stories as they were growing up.

On a more positive note, Rampo and Nanita also gave us wise old sayings as a way to perceive dilemmas and express common truths. Their *dichos* peppered every conversation. Whether serious or funny, these proverbs helped to explain or sum up a situation. Even as youngsters, we could quote *dichos* to fit any given occasion just as the grownups did. They were easy to remember because of their strong images and musical sound.

I later learned the English equivalents and realized that, while sometimes similar, they do not always use the same imagery. Some proverbs are very old phrases that don't make sense to most of us these days, but the meaning has not been lost. From the many I learned as a child, my favorite Spanish *dichos* and their meaning to me include:

A fuerza, ni los zapatos entran.

- You can't make a square peg fit into a round hole.

Al que madruga, Dios le ayuda.

- The early bird gets the worm, or, you snooze, you lose.

Del dicho al hecho, hay mucho trecho.

- It's easier said than done, or, actions speak louder than words

Él que tiene tienda, que la atienda, o si no, que la venda.

- Take care of what is yours; no one else will.

Más claro no canta un gallo.

- It's absolutely clear.

Mas vale tarde que nunca.

- Better late than never.

Mejor solo que mal acompañado.

- Better to be alone than in bad company.

No hay mejor espejo, que el amigo viejo.

- Good friends tell you the truth.

No falta un roto para un descocido.

- You can always find a companion in misfortune.

No todos los dedos de la mano son iguales.

- We are not all the same.

Panza llena, corazón contento.

- Full stomach, happy heart.

Querer es poder.

- Where there is a will, there is a way.

Chapter 23: A Night to Remember

Something terrible was going to happen.

Rampo looked at us with serious eyes and said with urgency, *"Vayan por los animales. Hoy, necesitan recogerlos y ponerlos adentro del granero temprano."* Junior and I had to bring the animals into the barn early, but why we didn't know.

It was a cold, cloudy afternoon, not the typical clear winter day to which we had become accustomed. His manner was as unusual as the weather. Junior whispered in my ear as we hustled around chasing the chickens back into the coop, *"¿Qué pasa con Rampo?"* What, indeed, was wrong with Rampo?

I replied with a little fear, *"No sé. No está sonriendo. Necesitamos hacer algo para hacerlo feliz."* Not knowing why he was not smiling, I felt it was our responsibility to cheer him up. I was concerned that we children had done something wrong. Something definitely was not right. We started dancing, giggling, and clowning around Rampo, but were left unrewarded with his usual smile. I told Junior that

Rampo must have something on his mind as we were not doing a very good job of cheering him up.

I knew that if I didn't pen all the chickens, we probably would miss finding their eggs in the bushes. So I dove after a particularly fast hen. Next came the cow to put into the barn, and lastly the horses. With some effort, we gathered all of the animals and tucked them in their shelters by early afternoon.

After seeing that the animals were secured, Rampo began picking up the tools and loose boards lying in the open or anywhere near the barn or corral. Since Rampo was not paying attention to our antics, we decided to make him laugh by peppering him with questions, trying to find what was wrong or if he was unwell, asking "*¿Rampo, hay algo mal? ¿Qué pasa? ¿No se siente bien?*" It was not his personality to be so serious with us; we were the sunshine of his life. But Rampo did not respond as we had hoped. He said he was fine and told us to go and play.

Instead, we ran into the house hoping to find out if Nanita would be more willing to talk and play. She always made time for her grandchildren, but today Nanita was in the same mood as Rampo. She too was quiet and pensive, very different from her usual talkative self. Instead of humming or whistling, which was her custom, she cooked almost in total silence and with the same sense of urgency shown by Rampo.

As soon as she finished, Nanita called us to the table, saying, "*Vengan a comer, hijitos. Quiero limpiar la cocina pronto.*" That was really odd. We never ate dinner this early! What was going on?

Shortly after, Rampo walked into the kitchen. We could smell the delicious aroma coming from a pot of pinto beans as Nanita finished making the *tortillas*. The smells alone made me hungry, even if it was only past midafternoon. We sat on the two *tarimas*, Rampo and Junior on one bench and Nanita and I on the other. "*Que bueno,*" said Rampo, praising Nanita's meal after each bite. He never forgot his manners.

Immediately after supper and with the sun barely setting, Rampo and Nanita took us to the *altarcito* in the living room to recite our nightly family prayers. Junior and I knew we had to be on our best behavior and hoped the dark feeling coming from our *abuelos* would fade away. Junior even withheld his usual jokes that made us laugh. Nanita started praying the Hail Mary in Spanish and we joined her on our knees with our hands folded in prayer.

> *Dios te salve, María. Llena eres de gracia.*
> *El señor es contigo. Bendita tú eres entre todas*
> *las mujeres y bendito es el fruto de tu vientre, Jesús.*
> *Santa María, madre de Dios. Ruega por nosotros*
> *pecadores. Ahora y en la hora de nuestra muerte. Amen.*

> Hail Mary full of grace, the Lord is with you.
> Blessed are you among women and blessed
> is the fruit of thy womb, Jesus. Holy Mary,
> mother of God, pray for us sinners now and
> at the hour of our death. Amen.

After prayers, Rampo told us to get ready for bed. "*Si,* Rampo," we said in unison as we stood up. We ran straight to bed. It was just getting dark and sleep was impossible. Additional questions plagued me: Why were our *abuelos* so stern today? Why was dinner early and why did they make us go to bed so early? I discussed these questions in whispers with Junior, so our *abuelos* wouldn't hear us from the other room.

Junior tried to change the subject by poking me. His cot and mine were so close together in the small bedroom that it was easy to fidget with each other. I laid in my bed wanting to figure it out before our *abuelos* went to bed. We all slept in the same room when just Junior and I were at the *ranchito*. Within a few minutes, after this active day, my eyelids got very heavy, and I fell asleep before Nanita and Rampo entered the room. Little did we know that the night would become an epic journey of survival that would be vividly retold to us at the beginning of every winter to demonstrate the strength and fortitude of our family.

It seemed that earlier in the day, my parents and Vera decided to travel to the *ranchito* after Papito closed his shoe shop in Las Vegas. Papito rarely came to the *ranchito*, but Mamita was not well; she could not raise her head from her pillow and even if she could, her head pounded with a blinding headache. This illness was very unusual for Mamita. No illness or pain ever stopped her from working. Even the severe varicose veins in her legs could not prevent her from working all day and into the evening to contribute to our family's meager income. So, there was a real reason for concern. Papito did not have money for a doctor and Vera did not know what to do for Mamita. They both knew Nanita would be the only person to help her. When snow began to lightly fall, they decided to head north immediately in an attempt to beat the impending spring snowstorm.

As if Mamita's illness was not enough to worry about, Papito had seriously injured his big toe after dropping a hammer on it at the shoe shop. It had become infected and he was in constant pain. Papito was very particular about his appearance, but the pain from the infection was enough to make him slice the top of his shoe to make room for his bandaged toe. His own injury also drove him to insist they leave for the *ranchito*. Papito was hoping for an herbal salve to ease his infection and pain.

As they drove towards Sapelló, the road changed from paved to gravel and then finally to clay dirt. As long as they were on the paved and graveled roads, the snow did not seem too bad. It had been warm enough that the snow melted as soon as it hit the road. When they reached the dirt road on the *mesa*, everything changed.

"Papito," Vera said with real concern, *"Que feo se puso. ¿De dónde vino la tormenta? Hace frío y ya no puedo ver por la ventana."* The storm had become bad enough that they were cold and could not see out of the car window.

The snow started coming down with a vengeance. It was as if all of heaven turned boxes of wet snow upside down and just dumped the contents down onto the earth. The heavy snow settled on the branches of the trees, bending them nearly down to the ground.

The dirt road seemed to have suddenly disappeared and the car began skidding, its tail swinging back and forth. Vera sucked in her breath and grabbed hold of the armrest, so she would not slam into Papito. She tried hard not to scream, not to let her parents know how scared she really was. Mamita laid in the back seat, never saying a word.

The swaying of the car gained momentum and soon they were off the road with just the front tires holding them from completely sliding down the hill. Papito got the car back on the road, but it went completely off the road again several times. Papito and Vera then had to get out of the car and push it back onto the road.

I could hardly imagine Vera helping to push. She was a very petite teenager and adults considered her delicate and fragile. Nonetheless, Vera did get out with the snow above her ankles to help Papito push the car. Once back on the road, they would kick the snow off their feet as best as they could and climb back into the car. Each time, they were wetter and colder than before, but they continued toward the *ranchito*.

By now, the inside of the car was as wet and muddy as the outside. The snow was coming down faster and heavier, the windshield wipers froze such that looking out the front windshield became impossible. The only solution was for Papito and Vera to open their side windows and stick their heads out to navigate and watch for the deep puddles of freezing mud and mounting snow.

The only conversation inside the car was Vera shrieking more than once, "*¡Cuidado!*" Dad, she would shout, you're too far to the right. There's a tree. Watch out!

He would ask her their direction, "*¿Puedes decirme a cuál dirección vamos?*" Vera would respond, "*Creo que el camino se va hacia la izquierda,*" guessing that they should go to the left.

Vera's knuckles were white from gripping the door handle as they swung back and forth. She found herself holding her breath and praying silently until Papito would talk to her about what she could see while he tried to control the car.

In the meantime, Mamita was getting colder with each passing moment. With the front windows rolled down, the wind and snow blew right into the back seat of the car. Her illness wouldn't allow her to generate heat any longer and Papito and Vera became more concerned with her well-being. They knew Mamita would never complain about her condition. I certainly never heard her say a word about her sacrifices for our family.

The question of turning back was never raised. They knew that the car could not turn around on the steep hillside and slippery road. Waiting out the storm was also not an option; the car had no heater. They had to keep moving forward or freeze.

Mamita was getting weaker and weaker. As the car swerved back and forth, she looked like a rag doll, swaying side to side and sometimes slamming into the front seat. She was sinking quickly and was no longer aware of their danger.

Papito muttered, *"Estamos casi en La Bajada. Si hacemos esa parte, lo habremos logrado. Entonces solo serán tres o cuatro millas más."* If they made it to the downhill section, they would be very close.

To Vera, it seemed longer. Early evening had turned into nighttime and the storm had turned the night pitch-black. They knew the worst was still ahead. It began with an S-curve down the steep hill of *La Bajada* and through an *arroyo*. On the other side of the *arroyo*, it was more hair-pin turns, and up another steep hill. As they had feared, when they got to the bottom of the hill, they got stuck in the *arroyo*.

This section of the road was a well-known and feared spot. Everyone got stuck there. If it had rained and the *arroyo* flooded, cars could not get across. Once the rain and flooding had passed, it would leave deep mud where cars got stuck. The only way out would be for the neighbors and their team of horses to pull out the unlucky car. It was here that Papito, Vera, and Mamita's hair-raising car ride ended.

Papito tried to drive the car through the *arroyo*, but it quickly got stuck. It was useless to continue trying. There was no way he could get enough momentum to get the car up the other side. The tires just spun deeper into the clay muck.

There was nowhere to go and nothing they could do.

Moreover, Papito's infected foot was much worse with the abuse it had endured each time he slammed on the brakes and went outside to push the car when it slipped off the road. When they turned to look at Mamita, they saw she was no longer moving. By the wisps of breath she expelled in the cold air, it appeared that she still was alive.

Vera was the only one who was able to go for help. Papito realized that Vera would be the only hope.

Despite his emotion, Papito kept his voice commanding, and told her to go to the *ranchito* for the horses: *"Vera, tienes que ir. Tienes que ir al rancho de tus abuelos para conseguir los caballos. Lo siento, Hija, pero la responsabilidad cae sobre ti. Mantente en la carretera y mantén la cabeza baja; la nieve no te golpeará en la cara tan fuerte. No importa que hagas, pero no te detengas."* Even as he knew that he was asking her to take on a huge responsibility, Papito also knew that they didn't have any other option. Their only hope was that Vera keep her head down and keep walking.

He and she both knew that, in order to get to our *abuelos'* house, she would have to cross a large creek. In a snow storm, it seemed like an impossible task. Trying to sound braver than she felt, Vera said, *"Bueno, Papito. Iré por Rampo. Estaré bien,"* reassuring him that she would be fine and would return with Rampo.

Death stared them in the face and dared Vera to back down; but somehow, she found her grit and set out. The snowflakes were so large and wet that she could hardly see in front of her. It was cold and windy, and the snow fell at an angle. The blackness of the night enveloped her as soon as she stepped out of earshot of her parents. She was so scared, she thought she heard screaming everywhere. The snow now was a couple of feet deep, and Vera could barely make her legs move. She was scared out of her wits.

There was no choice about which way she should go: forward, always forward. Going back meant she would have failed and she and her parents would be found days later frozen to death. Going forward might mean the same, but she only would allow herself to look ahead.

Vera continued to trudge ahead, but soon she no longer could see the road. The deafening silence was broken only by her heavy breathing and her sloshing through the wet heavy snow. Each step took much of her energy, while the snow's icy fingers seemed to grab at her legs and slow her pace. Vera tried to focus on her task by praying the Hail Mary aloud between her tears. As long as she heard herself praying, she was able to block the imaginary ghosts lurking in the darkness. Vera kept praying, despite her lungs burning from sucking in the cold air.

Vera walked for what seemed to be hours, never knowing if she was heading in the right direction. It was too dark and the snow too high to use the fence posts as a guide. She just kept walking, stumbling, picking herself up, and going again.

As she came over a hill, Vera heard what she thought was the howling of a pack of dogs coming toward her. Her imagination went wild. Was it something much worse? Coyotes? Wolves? Or some strange creature never before seen by man? Vera was a shivering mess of fear, but there was something familiar that instinctively made her go in the direction of the barking.

Vera's later reflections convinced her that the dogs had been sent to save her by God himself. Had she continued on to her grandparents, it would have been many more hours and chances are she never would have made it. Hearing the barking, she realized she was walking toward a neighbor who lived a few miles from her grandparent's *ranchito*. As the dogs rushed toward her, Vera imagined herself being eaten alive without ever telling anyone about her parents. The fear of the dogs made her tremble, even as the cold made her numb.

The great commotion caused the neighbor, Lalo, to go outside with a lantern to see what was upsetting the dogs. Vera was so weak from her arduous journey that she had little energy left to call out, but she managed to say just above a whisper, "*Lalo, aquí. ¡Ayúdanos! Estamos atascados.*"

The wind whisked her feeble cry for help toward Lalo and he finally heard her. For a moment, he stood stunned at what he saw. He shook his head, not believing his eyes. There fifty feet away from him stood a small shadow of a girl. She was drenched with the weight of her coat almost too much for her to bear. Her hair was hanging around her face stiff and frozen and her eyes were wide with fright. The urgency of her situation was plain to see, and his concern was immediate. Lalo ran to Vera and carried her inside their warm adobe house.

His wife, Celina, was looking out the window, wondering what was going on. As Lalo came in the door with this pitiful child, the commotion woke several of their children and added to the clamor of the baying dogs and weather outside. Celina immediately took charge of my frozen sister. Off came the dripping heavy coat and out came dry warm towels. The fire was quickly stoked in the kitchen stove and coffee was cooking. Vera kept trying to tell them that they had to save her parents, but they only paid attention to warming her until she had color back in her face.

Finally, with coffee in her cold body and stiffened fingers warmed from holding the cup, Vera was able to get out the story of their terrifying experience and the urgency of going back for her parents. A look passed between husband and wife. Lalo immediately went outside to gather the horses, saddle them, and gather whatever tools and ropes he needed to pull the car from its muddy grave. Celina in the meantime, gathered every spare blanket and even some off of the beds for him to take for Mamita and Papito. Lalo packed two horses and left with the lantern lit to search for the stranded couple.

Despite their long legs, the horses had trouble in the heavy snow; but they moved better than Vera. Lalo knew the road well since he often used it to go to town. With his horses being his family's only means of transportation, the horses instinctively knew the road too. Occasionally he would see signs of Vera's journey by where she had stumbled and fallen, but all signs of her footprints were buried by the snow and wind. Even knowing his way, having light, and seeing parts of Vera's trail to follow, Lalo felt lost several times before he finally found the larger road and knew he was headed in the right direction.

It took Lalo more than an hour to reach our parents. In daylight, and even if it snowed, it usually would take twenty minutes by horseback. Lalo claimed it was the most terrible blizzard he had ever seen and that it was one of the worst nights of his life, too.

When he found the car buried in the snow, my parents were nearly frozen. Lalo felt he could easily pull the car out of the mud because, as he said, he had wrenched many of these damned modern cars out of this infamous spot before. But as hard as the horses pulled and Lalo pushed, the car would not budge. It had snowed at least two feet and the road refused to give up the car.

Lalo and Papito finally realized that it was impossible to move the car. They feared that putting Mamita on one of the horses, given the elements and the lack of protection might make her condition worse. They both knew that doing so might cause her death.

But they had no choice. Carefully wrapping Mamita like a mummy, Papito climbed on a horse and Lalo lifted her and placed her in Papito's arms. As terrible as Papito felt, he found the strength to hold Mamita tightly all through the severe cold and darkness. Lalo grabbed the reins of Papito's horse and led the group back to his house.

God must have heard all of Vera's prayers because somehow the blizzard had changed direction and now the snow was blowing on their backs. They could see a little better and as a result made better time on their return.

There, Celina, Vera, and the kids were anxiously waiting. Vera was still scared from her journey and worried about her parents. When she heard the dogs howling, her heart raced, knowing it signaled the return of Lalo and hopefully her parents. She could barely get to the door fast enough. "*¡No, Vera!*" Celina called out, "*Espérate aquí. Te vas a enfermar y te vas a enfriar de nuevo.*" She did not want her to fall sick by getting cold again.

Celina tried to stop her as the snow and cold poured through the open door. In her efforts to confirm her parents were alive, Vera settled for yelling out and asking after Mamita, "*Mamita ¿estás bien?*"

When she saw Lalo and Papito struggling to take Mamita's wrapped and limp body down from the horse, Vera's heart went to her throat. Mamita was quickly taken inside and Lalo immediately turned away and went to tend the horses. He took off their gear and let them loose, so they could find their own shelter. He knew they wouldn't go far. They'd probably lean against the house until the storm let up.

To Vera's great relief, Papito and Celina unwrapped Mamita and they all saw her eyes blinking open. She was breathing. All Vera could muster through her tears was "*Gracias a Dios.*"

Papito and Mamita received the same treatment Vera did when she arrived. Knowing the night of terror was over, all three were able to finally lie down and rest. It was clear Mamita was out of her delirium because she told Papito that she did not want Nanita and Rampo to worry about them, knowing that they left Las Vegas in the brutal storm.

It took a long time for Vera to drift off to sleep. She continued to relive the night over and over, becoming more exhausted as she relived each trudging step. To take her mind off the nightmare, Vera feverishly prayed, thanking God for delivering all of them to safety. Eventually, her mind quieted and she fell asleep.

The next morning, the three awoke to a warm house. The deep snow of the night before sparkled like diamonds in the sun. Celina and Lalo had taken turns during the night keeping the fire burning, knowing their guests must not get chilled again. One of them had gone outside and scooped up snow, melting it on the stove for the morning coffee. Celina made fresh *tortillas* and added fresh coffee grounds to the old ones still in the kettle from the night before. The entire group relived the night's events while they drank their coffee, ate, and thanked God they were alive.

Around noon, Lalo was able to take the threesome on his horse-led wagon to my *abuelos'* house, which was about two miles from Lalo and Celina's home. Papito insisted on sitting up on the bench with Lalo, while Mamita, Vera, and several of the children rode in the back. Lalo had put the cover on the wagon so they were sheltered, but it was still cold and the snow made it difficult to travel.

Papito's car remained in the snow for a couple of days until a team of horses could pull it out. By then, many of the neighbors heard about the near-tragic event and pitched in to help move the car. Papito returned alone to Las Vegas. Before he left, however, Nanita gave him hot teas made of *yerba buena* and treated his sore toe with a salve of mashed yellow soap. Mamita and we three kids stayed at the *ranchito* for several more days. Nanita kept Mamita warm in bed, gave her hot teas, and placed sliced potatoes on her forehead and feet until her fever broke.

It was not until we woke up in the morning that Junior and I learned the reason for my *abuelos'* strange behavior the day before. While they were extremely concerned, they did not want to worry us about the impending snow storm and the possibility of Mamita, Papito, and Vera getting caught in a blizzard along the way. When Lalo drove his wagon to the *ranchito* in the afternoon, we were astonished to hear about Vera's role in saving our parents' lives.

The story of this epic adventure was re-told to us as *La Noche de la Gran Nevada*, The Night of the Giant Snowstorm. As the days passed and the neighbors heard what happened, it made quite an impression on old and young. Not only was a spring storm so unusual, but also the storm's severity was unheard of, even in winter. The most repeated part of the story, and what enthralled people most, was Vera's bravery and how she saved her parents lives. People wondered how an adult would have been able to survive the snow storm of the year, let alone a petite teenage girl. The story was repeated up and down the valley by all our neighbors and friends for years to come.

Over time, Vera was able to overcome most of the terror of that night. However, she would feel cold the rest of her life and said the haunting fear she felt while walking in the terrible storm would never leave her. So vivid was her experience that even in her later years, she would be able to recall every detail, every sound, and every snowflake that fell on that fateful night. Junior and I were in awe of our sister and hoped that we would be as brave as she and weather any storm.

Adios

Chapter 24: The Last Goodbye

Spring in northern New Mexico was a time of hope and renewal.

At the *ranchito*, it was plowing season and time to get the fields ready. Rampo had hitched the horses to the plow and was now guiding them across his fields to loosen the soil. Junior and Cunde, followed behind and moved the unearthed rocks to the sides of the fields so that they wouldn't interfere with the ground leveling that Rampo would undertake before planting. I stood leaning on the fence, under a tree, watching them work and enjoying the wonderful smell newly-released from the moist earth.

It was an extremely hot day. The sun beat down. All three wore their wide brimmed straw hats, but I could see that they frequently took off their hats and wiped their brows with their red bandanas.

Around noon, Rampo moved the horses to plow the last field. It was the one closest to the apple orchard and quite near the house. He always left that one for last. He told the boys to go play while he finished up the last few turns around the field before breaking for lunch.

The boys immediately took off toward the nearby creek with their ever-ready BB guns, which they had left near the fence earlier in the morning. They quickly ran and shot their guns into the air a few times. Then they amused themselves by thrusting their hands into the shallow creek to see if they could grab a fish while at the same time cooling their arms and faces. Every once in a while, we checked to see if Rampo had stopped working because that would be the signal to go in to eat lunch.

When Rampo finished leveling the last field, he motioned to the three of us to start toward the house. He then guided the horses off the field and harnessed them to a wagon to take them to the corral. We did not hurry after he called us; we knew it would take Rampo time to tend to the horses. The boys continued to chase each other and goof off in general as they meandered toward the house.

Suddenly we heard Nanita frantically screaming at the top of her lungs for us to come quickly. She was yelling something about Rampo, but we could not understand her. We finally heard hear her scream, *"Vengan. Rampo se ha caído."*

We ran as fast as we could, while Nanita continued screaming that Rampo had fallen down between the house and the tack room. When we got there, it was a scene we would never forget. We thought Rampo was just sitting on the ground, resting his back on the right front wheel of the wagon. But that was an odd place to sit and the horses were still harnessed. Don, the horse on the right kept turning his head to look at Rampo, whose left leg was a few inches from his own right rear leg. Had Don spooked, he would have crushed Rampo's leg.

When we got closer to Rampo, we noticed that his eyes were closed, and he was sitting motionless with a hand over the silver cross he wore on a leather string around his neck. Nanita was now hugging him and sobbing that the last sound he made was when he had kissed his cross.

Our Rampo was gone. He must have died instantly of a heart attack. As Nanita cried, she implored the saints to pray for his soul and asked why this had to happen. She was beside herself. Nanita had just lost her partner of a lifetime. She was eighteen years of age and he was twenty when they married. They were each other's life.

Some of the closer neighbors heard Nanita's screams. We could see them running quickly up and down the narrow dirt paths leading to the house. Benito, the closest neighbor, was the first to arrive. With his help, he and the boys unhitched the horses to move them away from Rampo's body. Junior remembers that before the horses stepped away, they flinched, turned their heads around as if to say goodbye to Rampo, and then gently moved forward without touching him.

Celina, our other neighbor, had now arrived and wailed, *"Don Silviano no nos dejes,"* asking Rampo not to leave us. Nanita stirred to her senses and told Benito, Junior, and Cunde they needed to go to Sapelló. They were to use the phone at the store and notify the authorities and our parents in Las Vegas. Benito was willing to go, but said he did not know how to drive. My brother piped up that he could drive, although he had never driven in his life. They had no choice, so the three ran down the road and crossed the creek to where the car was parked. Due to a recent flood, Rampo had left the car on the other side so it would not get stuck in the muck.

Between the three of them, they managed to start the car and make it safely down the dusty road and across the hills.

Benito drove behind the wheel, Junior told Benito when to press the clutch, and he shifted the gears with Cunde shouting when to turn the wheel to keep it on the road.

It took a while, but they made it to the grocery store in Sapelló, which had the only telephone in the area. The storeowner quickly called the coroner's office. He was told that it would be two to three hours before the coroner could get to the *ranchito*. The coroner apparently had to prepare the funeral paper work, find a hearse, and round up a jury to witness the signing of the death papers before leaving. The coroner also insisted that Benito, Junior, and Cunde wait for him in Sapelló to guide him to the ranch. That was a good idea because there were no signs or visible markers leading to the *ranchito*.

While waiting for the telephone calls to be completed, someone offered Junior a coke because he had just mentioned that it was his tenth birthday. He had never had a coke before, but he swallowed the whole bottle in one gulp; a grownup would probably have had a strong drink to settle his nerves.

When the authorities finally arrived at Sapelló, Cunde rode with them in the hearse to show them the way, a second car full of men followed behind. Junior and Benito drove Rampo's car at the tail end of the procession. It was pitch dark before the coroner and the rest of the group arrived at the *ranchito*. Mamita, Papito, and Vera would not get to the *ranchito* until much later.

By law, no one could move the body until the coroner allowed it. Nanita was plenty upset that her beloved Rampo had to lay on the ground all that time. Her loving neighbors surrounded her and tried to console her as best as they could until the authorities appeared.

Once there, the coroner inspected Rampo's body by the light of coal oil lanterns and declared him dead of natural causes. He then turned to Nanita to ask her a few questions, and had her complete a long legal-looking form that none of us understood. The coroner finally announced that Rampo's body could be moved. Nanita, Junior, and I rushed to his body, tearfully hugging and caressing each other and him. I lost my voice, but my head screamed with questions: How could this be? What would we do without Rampo? Who was going to love us as much as he loved us? Did he know how much I loved him?

I was frozen on my knees and could not take my eyes off Rampo.

A woman neighbor cried and wailed as loudly as Nanita and the rest of us. Amongst the sadness, the *vecinos'* prayers were constant. Some were started by one person and others would join in a chanting voice. Rosaries were recited with soft cries. You could hear both loud and quiet appeals to God. It seemed like neighbors were everywhere standing, kneeling, huddling together, or touching Rampo. Men tried to hold back their tears, but the constant blowing of their noses gave their feelings away. Everyone was touched; all loved Rampo.

Nanita eventually finished cleaning Rampo's face and hands, while talking to him and praying between loud and soft grief-stricken sobs. One neighbor started singing a hymn and others prayed:

Ábransele las puertas del cielo,
alégrense con él los ángeles;
Recíbele, Señor, en tu reino.
Rueguen por él todos los Apóstoles.

Open for him the doors of Heaven,
May all the angels with him be joyful,
Greet him, Lord, to your Kingdom,

May all the Apostles pray for him.

After some time, Nanita got up and went with the neighbors inside the house to fetch the last clothes Rampo would wear. For his funeral, it could only be his best blue suit, white shirt, and tie. Someone hitched Don and Whitey to the wagon. When all was ready, Rampo was placed on the wagon pulled by his horses. We followed behind in a second wagon, holding on to each other and sobbing. On that dark night, we heard the hooting of an owl marking the loss of our loved one.

When we crossed the muddy creek, Rampo was transferred, along with his carefully wrapped clothes, into the hearse for the long slow ride to Las Vegas where funeral arrangements would be made. He would be buried in his family home town of San Antonio, now called upper Las Vegas.

We did not realize that it would also be our last time at our enchanting *ranchito*. Nanita could not envision herself living there without Rampo and never returned to her cherished home. Neighbors brought her precious *altarcito* and a few clothes, but she did not want anything else. She came to live with us in Las Vegas and immediately sold our beloved *ranchito*.

Mamita's safe haven for her children seemed lost. She could not fathom that the magical times we spent with Nanita and Rampo would have a powerful, lasting impact on the three of us grandchildren. The sacred seeds of faith and community, of the passion for learning and the love of the land, would remain with us forever.

Mi Gran Familia

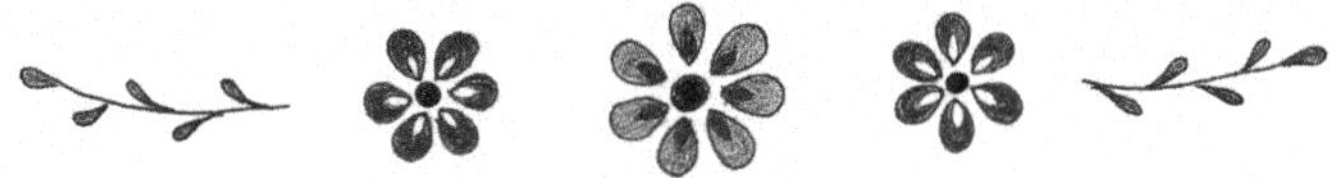

More about my family and community.

Papito

Papito was a remarkable man in many ways.

Maurilio Antuna was born in the town of Durango, Mexico during the Mexican Revolution of 1910 to 1920. Orphaned at a young age, Papito was forced to learn many skills. Lucky for him, he had a talent for music and was enlisted as a bugler for Pancho Villa.

Seeking more adventures, he taught himself to play the trumpet and joined a Mexican circus. At sixteen years of age, he crossed into the United States with the circus. During a stop in Las Vegas, New Mexico, Papito fell in love with the village and saw work opportunities.

He left the circus and started a small shoe shop and musical groups for the many community festivals in the area. Papito was full of confidence. Maybe it was because of his education and the skills he acquired during his "worldly" travels. It didn't hurt that he was a very handsome man. He was tall, thin, and dark-skinned with a mop of curls and a perfectly trimmed moustache. And he always dressed in the finest of clothes.

In no time, he became well known for his fine leather craftsmanship and the great pride he took in his appearance. At the shop he wore denim pants with a matching shirt under his beige cobbler's apron. While his hands always looked stained from the shoe polish he worked with all day, his *delantal y ropa*, his apron and clothes, were immaculately clean.

When hanging around town, Papito would dress smartly in a white shirt with a tie, a business suit, and polished *botines*, boots that he made himself. He also wore special outfits when playing with his band. Along with his starched white shirt, he wore *una corbata de moño*, a crossbow ribbon tie, a vest or a jacket lined along the edges with red or grey stripes, and a matching red or grey band hat that had a small attached visor. Papito wore his band hat slightly cocked to one side so that a curl of his hair would fall below the slanted side of the cap. He was quite the looker!

Papito was playing at a local dance when he met Mamita. She had gone to a community dance with her many older sisters. One look at my dad, the handsome trumpet player on the bandstand, and Mamita was smitten. Papito also took notice of the youngest and most beautiful of the sisters. After one of the dance sets, he descended from the bandstand to ask her to dance. It was not unusual for band members to leave the group and dance with their girlfriends or wives. They would also go and greet friends or family after playing a song. The band, community musicians who had played together for years, easily continued playing with the available musicians.

It did not take long for romance to blossom and before too long the entire community took notice. Papito was considered an outsider who spoke a different Spanish. In the tight northern New Mexican Hispanic community, all strangers were eyed carefully; strangers who were men were especially not trusted with their beautiful women.

Papito and Mamita continued to see each other when possible at public places with her sisters in tow. It was extremely difficult for the two to meet at all because the family had gotten wind of the budding romance and did what they could to keep them apart. Mamita's parents didn't know his family and, most disturbing of all, they found out that he was an atheist. You can imagine the shock. Mamita's family was very religious, so the family definitely considered him not to be a good prospect as a future son-in-law. But, the love of my soon-to-be parents won out and they married. And yes! The wedding took place in a church; He probably had to go to confession to be married.

Regardless, Papito remained a poor lost soul in the eyes of my family. He reminded everyone that during the Mexican Revolution he was sent to an orphanage at age eleven and suffered so much there that he lost his faith in God. Papito saw religion as social control and reminded us children of it every time we went to church with Mamita.

After their wedding, Papito and Mamita set up a home in a two-room house on the west side of Las Vegas. A few years later, he moved his shoe shop business to a busier location on the east side of town. With a growing business, he bought Mamita a slightly larger adobe house to fit their growing family.

Papito would remind us that he was the provider of the family, but actually he fell short in his role as a caretaker. He used most of his money on himself and for what he called his "business expenses," which meant clothes, musical instruments, and a car. He seemed to have little left to feed and dress his family. Alone with us kids, Mamita learned to live with little food, no electricity, gas, or running water. Papito always said to us, *"La próxima semana va a estar mejor."* We so wanted to believe him that the next week would be better!

Mamita tried to keep her marital problems from us, but even as small children we were aware that something was very wrong.

Papito was gone a lot from home. Mamita would make up excuses for him such as he slept at the shoe shop because he worked late, or he played in the band late at night and that is why we would not see him for dinner. On many Sundays, when he came home, we were told not to make any noise because Papito was asleep after having been out all night. Mamita would whisper, *"No hagan ruido."* We were told not to make noise when Papito was around. Obviously, Papito was not active in our world and seemed far removed when he did spend time with us.

When we visited my mother's parents in Las Manuelitas, our relationship with him did not change much. We usually found him reading a book under a tree, as far away from our family as possible. Sometimes he played the guitar outside on my grandparents' patio and sang beautiful songs. On these occasions in the courtyard, we would learn songs he liked that we had never heard before.

When Papito was with the family or at another nearby ranch, he mostly conversed with Rampo or the male neighbors. I don't recall him having many conversations with Nanita, Mamita, or us children. At other times he napped, or at least he looked to me like he was sleeping, so we would not disturb him.

Regardless of his actions toward Mamita and us children, Papito was a brilliant man in my eyes. He never formally studied English, but seemed to have mastered the language. He educated himself by reading about a number of topics in both English and Spanish. He was a scholar who studied until he had a profound understanding of the subject. Indeed, Papito was a master artist, electrician, carpenter, musical composer, teacher, and inventor of all kinds of gadgets. There was nothing he could not tackle.

He made sure we children read all the time too. Throughout my life, I wished many times that he would have spent more time with us and shared his other talents. But that changed as I grew older. While he shared his passion for reading and a hunger to learn, I came to understand that his *machismo* and sense of masculine superiority would not allow him to see his wife or his children as equals.

His self-indulgence and other faults did not bother me. I accepted whatever he cared to give us. Besides, I had other wonderful people in my life who reached out to me, nourished my heart and soul with faith, and encouraged me to succeed in all my endeavors.

Mamita

Mamita was a strikingly tall and beautiful woman.

She possessed thick flowing brown hair that enhanced her fair complexion and naturally rosy cheeks. At five-feet, five-inches, she towered over most of the young women in Las Vegas, New Mexico. Little wonder that Mamita caught the attention of Papito.

Many people considered Mamita the picture of serenity and beauty. Some thought Mamita was shy, but I believe it was just part of her reserved and thoughtful nature not to initially engage with others. Mamita often told us her favorite *dicho*, *"En boca cerrada no entre mosca."* Following her own advice, Mamita considered silence to be golden and seldom talked with adults past the expected traditional greeting of *Buenos días*.

Even though she only had a seventh grade education, she believed passionately in studying and learning. We heard daily that a good education would remove us from the dismal poverty in which we lived. When staying at our grandparents' *ranchito*, she encouraged us to read Rampo's periodicals in either Spanish or English. We read the newspaper *La Voz del Pueblo* and *Farmer's Almanac*. Sometimes we read out loud to her and sometimes to ourselves. She even gave us writing exercises to describe the changing beauty of plants and nature at the *ranchito* and in Las Vegas.

Whenever we got out of hand or acted up, Mamita would tell us to play school. This game meant practicing reading and writing in English, but sometimes she would have us play school in Spanish. I loved school, so this was a game I happily played.

Although she wasn't much into telling jokes, her quiet, radiant smile would tell us how much she enjoyed our humor. A pat on the head further confirmed to us that she thought we were funny when we told a joke or did something that made her smile. She loved us children and hugged, kissed, and patted us on the head constantly. We three children loved her back and through her actions we came to love and care for each other.

If we were seated or lying at her feet, she would rub our scalp with her fingers. These mini head massages felt so good and soothing. Even though my brother and I were young, we realized that we had to do with less and less as we got older, because Papito could not or would not provide us with enough money for our growing needs. Mamita would remind us that we were just as good, and maybe even smarter, than children who had much more than we did. She instilled in us that we had good brains, and, if we did well in school, we would earn a good living. She was a top teacher, and we were the lucky students. Lucky, indeed!

Mamita also had beautiful manners and did her best to pass them along to us children, even when we were being rascals at the *ranchito*. She reflected the skills she learned from an outstanding teacher who had taught her to behave with dignity and to have a heart of gratitude. She never hesitated to help the neighbors with their children if they needed to leave and run an errand. Mamita would also put her work aside and teach the young girls in the community how to crochet and knit. I'll never forget Mamita's saying *"El favor bien hecho o nada,"* because she herself was a role model that one should do a favor well or not at all.

Her teacher also had shown Mamita how to sew beautifully. Mamita used her sewing skills – even with very little money – to turn our own *casita* into an enchanting setting. She covered cardboard boxes with whatever material she could find and made them into coffee and side tables. She crocheted the ends of curtains and made them look like lace. She sewed designs on our quilts and made them appealing for us kids.

Mamita insisted that we just had to be more creative with what little we had. Mamita was a master creator. Anything she touched – the food we ate, the clothes she made, and the decorations she designed for our *casita* – became elegant. I so wanted to be like Mamita!

Mamita could also turn trash into functional art. I recall her sitting on Nanita's porch with piles of Sunday comics that she had collected from friends who received newspapers. She cut and pasted the colored sections into small cone-shaped hollow beads, strung the beads on individual strings, and hung them as privacy curtains between our rooms since we had no doors. The curtains of beads were so vivid and lively to see. They were a great toy for us kids to race through as they clacked back and forth.

Another passion of Mamita's was her gardening. Although her plants started as slips given to her by neighbors or friends, she knew how to root and nurture them until they bloomed.

All over our *casita*, dozens of glass jars held begonias, impatiens, lilacs, roses, and sweet peas.

When there weren't fresh flowers to cut and bring home from the *ranchito*, Mamita improvised by creating bouquets from dead grasses and little greenish twigs. In early spring, she brought home dandelions and a few tiny elm tree branches that had started to green. Mamita often said, "*Todo se puede hacer lindo. Toma tiempo y un poco de paciencia.*" This *dicho* was definitely true of Mamita: With time and a little patience, she could make anything beautiful.

Whenever she had time to sit, Mamita would crochet. She spent many hours crocheting string or any thread she came upon. That activity resulted in her constantly suffering from a tender and bruised finger. Papito took pity on her condition and made a soft leather thimble for her sewing finger. He ingeniously added two leather strings for Mamita to wrap around her hand and secure the thimble. It actually worked, and the thimble never fell off her finger again.

When we had a little extra money to buy thread or if someone gave her a spool, she would crochet exquisite doilies and tablecloth edgings. If someone asked her to crochet for them, she could make bigger pieces. Each time, Mamita used tiny perfect stitches. She once made a foot-wide edging for a long altar tablecloth at our church. If ever she found a dropped stitch, she would unwind and start all over again. After the crocheting was perfect, she spent hours shaping the doilies. She first put them into thick sugar water and then molded them until they became sculptured masterpieces. She would tell us, "*Si tuviéramos almidón, tal vez podría hacerlos más rápido. Pero el azúcar realmente funciona bien. ¿No crees?*" What did we know about the advantage of using starch over sugar to set the doilies? Of course, we agreed with anything Mamita asked us.

If Mamita had embroidery thread, and often her neighbors gave her some, she embroidered everything she could get her hands on: kitchen towels, pillow cases, the tops of sheets, bedspreads, blouses, cushions, and on and on. She loved to embroider as much as to crochet. She embroidered over the big Indian head and the bouquet of roses that were printed on a couple of flour sacks. Once she waited to buy a sack of flour that had a pretty picture on it. She said the sacks were perfect embroidery material. A scrap of cloth was never wasted, for, as Mamita would recite to us when working, *"Nada se gasta."*

She was also an artist with cloth. She cut every small piece of material she found into narrow strips. She used them to make colorful rag rugs. With her crochet hook, she inserted each strip close together into a large square of gunny cloth. Mamita hand-tied each piece, so it would withstand lots of use and many washes. What a treat to get out of bed in a cold room and have your feet snuggle into those cozy rugs. It was pure heaven!

She cut the bigger scraps into squares of all sizes to make patchwork quilts. That was the only kind of blanket we had. Occasionally, if we had a little money, she would buy a flannel sheet for one side of her beautiful patchwork. Most often, she would put a worn blanket between the newer material before she quilted it. Doing so made the quilts thick and toasty warm. Some blankets had three or four worn blankets inside the new ones to make them extra heavy. Once under such a blanket, you could hardly move. Drifting off to sleep, we could count on Mamita whispering to us, *"¿Están calientitos? Duérmanse, mis angelitos."* I don't know that we were angels, but we were definitely warm.

Most amazing to me was that Mamita sewed all these items by hand. I can still hear her voice counting. She counted six stitches and then would sew two stitches backwards, so the seam would never come undone. She would let us know, *"Así duran para siempre."* It was a real chore when we had to undo one of her seams. She wasn't kidding: They were as tough as a machine sewn seam and lasted forever.

Because of her deep faith in God, she prayed often and made sure we learned traditional Catholic prayers. She normally had a rosary in her apron pocket, but prayed only in the mornings and before going to bed. As her marriage broke apart, we could hear her pleading with the Lord to protect her family.

Using her imagination, Mamita stretched our food with water and flour. She also made sure we never looked "dirt poor." Mamita would scrub us until we hurt. She washed, sewed, and ironed our clothes to make sure we looked clean in public. She also kept a clean and inviting house.

Mamita strongly believed that God would come to our rescue. While waiting for this miracle, she dealt with poverty in very direct ways. She would remind us not to tell anyone we were poor. Mamita would say to be proud of our good grades and always to be polite and kind to others. She also reminded us to be grateful for our talented father. All this achievement, she said, should be enough to replace the lack of money.

As we children grew, she knew it would take more than faith and her talents to raise the three of us. Out of desperation, Mamita reached out to her adoptive parents, Juanita and Silviano Tafoya. They would be the miracle for which she prayed.

Hermanita

Elvira Antuna, or Vera as I liked to call her, was my *hermanita.*

She was petite and fine boned with short, dark, and wavy hair. As she was seven years older than I, my first clear memories of Vera were during her teenage years.

I clearly remember Vera hating to go to the *ranchito,* unlike Junior and I. When it was announced that the family was going to our *abuelos'* house, she would whisper to me so the grownups wouldn't hear, that she had a date and would have to break it. She would sigh and mention the boy's name, and then ask me not to tell our parents. I understood we were having a grownup talk and would pat her like Mamita patted me on the head when I was sad.

Vera was always the last one to appear and sulked when something needed to be done. She simply did not like physical work. If someone tried to get her to help, she would respond, "Rampo always says, *No todos los caballos nacen para la guarnición.*" Vera liked this *dicho.* She was definitely not a horse to be harnessed. She also didn't mind reminding everyone that she was sickly as a child and now too small and fragile to work.

Even though I was many years younger, I was much taller than Vera and felt motherly toward her because of her short stature and general weakness. I truly believed she couldn't carry or lift anything heavy or do any kind of manual labor. I also couldn't imagine her using her tiny, pretty hands to pull thorny weeds or to plunge in the dish water.

My mothering nature often led me to do Vera's chores. Nanita and Mamita would look at each other with smiles as I raced to finish my chores of sweeping, gardening, or washing clothes in order to go and help Vera. They would tell me, "*¡Ah! Qué mi hijita. Siempre la mamá.*" They thought it was charming that the younger daughter acted the mother and wanted to do Vera's share of the work. But I thought of it as grownup work and felt honored to cover for my sister.

Besides, it was important for Vera to return to her book or magazine. She was always reading, just like Papito, but she read movie magazines that she hid from the grownups. Because she trusted me not to tell, I was rewarded with being able to peek over her shoulder. It was fun looking at the pretty women and handsome men. She sometimes let me role-play with her as if we were the actors.

Vera would say, "*Ven, hermanita.* Let's pretend we're movie stars. I'll be Carole Lombard." When she wanted me to play with her, she would call me, Come little sister. As she put down the movie magazine she had been devouring, I recognized the dreamy look in her eyes and knew I was going to be invited to share her latest fantasy of Hollywood and the rich, rich people.

I excitedly scrambled around the yard looking for a twig, so I could use it as a cigarette. "You be Rita Hayworth," she said with a flick of her hand. "Let's pretend that we are going to a party." I was honored to be part of her dream world. I had no clue as to who these people were or how they lived. It was a world away from me, but I took my cues from Vera. She wrapped her pretend fur around her shoulders and, with a flip of her head, caused her wavy bangs to gracefully change sides. She would then say in her exotic Hollywood accent, "Come on, Darling. Let's go!" And off we went in our pretend limousine.

I didn't know much about movie stars, but Vera was crazy about them, so I knew I should like them too. She told me that besides being very beautiful, they ate whatever they wanted and anytime they wanted, even bananas and ice cream. I just couldn't imagine such a world. At our home, we lived mostly on *tortillas*, beans, chili, and seasonal vegetables.

Vera also told me that the movie stars had beautiful clothes that cost lots of money. She would explain about how they had tons of high-heeled shoes. Some were even open-toed and had ankle straps. "Imagine," she would say, "These shoes are all the rage. I wish I had a pair." I'd then join in and sigh, "I wish I had a pair, too." We would promptly rise up on our toes and gracefully tiptoe around the dirt yard. Vera and I looked glamorous in our imaginary high heels, until our feet ached.

Other times, Vera would act as if she knew the actors personally. One day she said, "Oh, my gosh, I don't believe it. That is so sad!" She spoke with so much emotion that I thought she was going to bust wide open. "What? What's wrong?" I asked urgently. "They're getting divorced," she replied with a big sigh. I knew this news was bad by how shocked she was, but I didn't know what it meant. I had heard the word once or twice on Sundays at church during the priest's sermon, but never questioned it. I just figured it was another fancy English word. After hearing Vera use the word, I got the courage to ask her what it meant. Using her teacher's voice, Vera answered, "That's when a man and woman go different ways because they are no longer in love. You know, like if Mamita told Papito to go away because she did not love him anymore." I didn't understand the example at all. Why would Mamita tell that to Papito? Why would a divorce make them go different places? It was probably more of that grownup thinking of hers.

The magazines her friends loaned her also had pictures of movie stars. The women had their hair done very differently than ours. It was soft and smooth with waves that seemed unnaturally placed to me. I was accustomed to my long heavy braids and, while Vera was always in style, even her hairdo was simple compared to that of the glitzy movie stars.

Whenever Vera turned the page of a magazine and saw a picture of Clark Gable, she would place her hand immediately over her heart and, at the same time, dramatically let out an exclamation as she pretended to faint. Then while she fanned the heat from her face, she would tell me, "He's the most handsome man in the world! Just perfect." For the life of me, I could not imagine anyone more perfect than Jesus; but, then, what did I know about my sister's grownup world? Nanita thought Jesus was very beautiful, and I did too. Did "beautiful" and "handsome" mean the same? Oh, the grownup world was so hard to understand for a ten year-old. There were too many words I could not grasp in either English or Spanish.

Vera's appetite for movie stars did not end with her reading. Her love of movie stars led her to name all our chickens at the *ranchito* with movie star names. She named the hens Hedy Lamarr and Betty Grable. On the roosters she bestowed names such as Cesar Romero and Clark Gable.

Ever the teacher, Vera spent hours teaching us the names and made sure we matched them to the right chicken. We thought it was great fun, and she seemed so happy that we were extra good students.

Vera wanted so much to look like the movie stars in the magazines. With help from Mamita, Vera actually dressed just like one. Mamita did it by taking hand-me-downs from our neighbors and making them into sophisticated dresses. My favorite was a green princess style dress with a Peter Pan collar. It complimented her olive-colored skin so nicely. Mamita even made a gorgeous hat out of the same material to match Vera's dress. The hat was cone-shaped and covered with a little loose veil. Vera completed the outfit by wearing our cousin Frances' Cuban-heeled shoes. It was so funny to watch my sister totter in her high-heels. While I already had feet that would fit her shoes, I was still too young to share in that dramatic world.

Besides knowing so much about Hollywood actors, Vera knew about many other things from her readings and would share whatever she discovered. Vera was the only one at home who really knew how to speak English. No wonder we always asked her to be the teacher; our real teachers only spoke English and Vera modeled them to perfection. Little did Junior and I know then that Vera's lessons would give us an advantage in learning English.

Another obsession of Vera's was dancing. When at the *ranchito*, she would crank up the Victrola and dance with our brother and me on the big porch. She could spin around like a top and keep great rhythm. The trouble was she wanted to teach us the Charleston and the new dances, but we only had records of Spanish music, so it didn't work very well. That type of dancing went on only when adults were not present; otherwise we danced the polka and other steps

Nanita had taught us. The type of dancing Vera loved seemed to be forbidden, just like the movie star magazines. She was caught between our parents' and grandparents' world and her siblings' childish behavior.

Despite our difference in age and interests, we were very close. Our family situation was partly the reason for our closeness, but our lifestyle contributed to our nearness as well. At home in Las Vegas, my sister and I shared the same bed and our baby brother mostly slept with Mamita in her room. We had joint ownership of the hairbrush, our hair ribbons, and even clothes. Mamita would remake dresses that were given to us, first for Vera, then later to fit my long skinny body. As the years progressed, it wasn't just the space and things we had to share. It was everything! We truly loved each other's companionship.

Vera would tell us she could hardly wait to graduate from high school and strike out on her own. That was going to be a special feat. No one from our home or extended family had even gone to high school, but Vera's passion for reading and interest in the world outside Las Vegas helped her to succeed. She accepted a teaching job at a local rural school at age seventeen, when she was just out of high school. In her spare time, Vera studied to be a secretary and found work with several businesses in New Mexico and then in California. She later was hired as an executive secretary at the Sandia National Laboratories in Albuquerque and worked there until her retirement. Throughout her career, Vera always made time to care for Nanita, Mamita, Junior, me, and later my three children. She never forgot us, even while she used education to leap beyond the *ranchito* and Las Vegas.

HERMANITO

As the youngest child and only son, Maurilio Antuna was loved by all of us.

He was born with the good looks of both my parents. From Mamita, he inherited light coloration and rosy cheeks. His height and natural charm came from Papito. We always said with pride, *"Mi hermanito es lindo."* He looked like the pictures of handsome little boys in the magazines, only he had dark straight hair instead of the usual blond curly locks. My sister and I thought he looked like an angel. In addition to being just plain cute, he was a well-mannered child. And we all knew he was Mamita's favorite. That did not bother us two girls; he was our favorite too.

Somewhere between my brother's age of six or seven, my sister and I, who now knew English, changed his Spanish name to "Junior". When enrolled in the first grade, the teachers who knew no Spanish and could not pronounce his given name, accepted our English nickname for him. They even used it in his report cards and other school records.

After school each day, Junior loved following me around since I was two years older than him. He would tag along, and we would spend hours playing together. Sometimes we would seek out Vera, who didn't always like the things Junior and I did, but she did join in our games. Several times, Vera and I dressed Junior in some of our clothes and thought he was the sweetest child that ever lived. He was not happy to play dress-up, but did it to stay in our company.

As Junior got older, it was clear he needed a friend. Luckily for him, he found one close by to my *abuelos' ranchito* in Las Manuelitas. His name was Cunde, and Junior looked forward to playing with him when we were at the *ranchito*.

"*¡Ay viene Cunde!*" Junior would yell as soon as he saw his best friend coming down the winding path from his house. By now Cunde had crossed the río and was near the orchard close to our *abuelos'* house. Cunde was tiny in stature, but we thought most ranch kids were mature beyond their years, even if they were smaller than we were. They weren't afraid of anything that might come along their path.

Junior would jump up with glee and run down the path from the *ranchito* house to meet Cunde. He'd talk to himself, making plans as he jumped, "*Vamos a jugar con los trompos.*" The boys played tops and many other games until it was time for Cunde to return home before sunset.

Sometimes Junior did things he wasn't supposed to do. Vera and I would cover for him. We'd say he wasn't aiming to hit the chicken, or the side of the barn, or whatever he had hit. We would argue that all little boys on ranches threw rocks and Junior wasn't any different. It was obvious that Junior loved to throw rocks and had a pretty good aim that got better before he got much older.

By the time he was eight, he and Cunde were into BB guns. Both were great shots, but many things were off limits.

They couldn't shoot birds, but they could shoot the ones that carried our chickens away. They so wanted to prove their shooting skills, but were limited to throwing cans up high in the air and bringing them down with their shots. They actually got good at it. Rampo would say, "*¡Son buenos con los rifles!*" I later learned from the boys that someone who was good at shooting a rifle was called a crack shot. Regardless, I was afraid of guns and would never even hold one. I was teased as the "fraidy cat," but never changed my attitude.

The boys also rode our fat, slow horses. Although Cunde was a good horse rider and could even ride bareback on any horse he could catch, he was content riding our horses with Junior. They were great friends. Occasionally Cunde's older brother, Cruz, would join them. However, he was usually busy with chores and couldn't play very long.

Cunde gave my brother and me lessons on how to mount a horse. I'll never forget the first time when Cunde said, "*Deténganse de la clin.*" Junior caught on fast; he understood how to hold on to the mane of the horse. I had a hard time learning. I felt that pulling on the mane would hurt the horse, and it might buck me off. It also made me think of my own long hair, which hurt when pulled. I knew there had to be a better way to mount the poor horses and it turned out that there was. I later learned that if the horse had a bridle and reins, I could swing my leg over the horse and stay on top of it.

My brother also learned how to handle ropes much better than I. Darn, that rope always burned my hands! No lassoes for namby-pamby me. Why wasn't I born physically strong? I doubted myself as I grew up. I never could challenge anyone physically. I was even afraid of baseballs coming at me: I ducked and closed my eyes. I had to find safer games for amusement.

Junior was clever at fixing things, just like my father. He would make do with whatever was at hand. He would use old screws, old nails, wire, string, anything to fix toys or sometimes grownup things. He was smart and could make anything.

My brother and I seldom quarreled. Maybe we argued about who would play with the blue marble or who got the top that was the best spinner. Our disagreements rarely reached a loud shouting stage before Mamita would intervene. Besides, I usually lost the quarrel given that I was older than Junior, and was told that I should have more sense.

In most cases, Junior got his way and that seemed to create peace in the family. I was learning that boys were always right, especially in traditional Hispanic households. But worst of all, I was not being taught to hold my own in an argument. This important lesson definitely was overlooked and was something I had to learn as an adult.

Usually the youngest was the favorite of the moment, until the new child arrived. In several of the homes up the valley, there was a baby every year. But not at my house: Junior was our baby forever.

By the time Junior entered high school, he was over six feet in height with rugged good looks that made every woman stop and stare. My sister and I decided a name change was in order to match his looks, so we renamed him "Bud." He never did pick up the passion for reading, but he was multi-talented just like my father. Seeking his independence at an early age, Bud left home before finishing high school and joined the navy. He became a Naval Chief Petty Officer and explored the world. Later he married and went on to develop into a master handyman, computer whiz, and successful real estate developer. Bud remained our favorite talented and loving brother!

¡Y Yo!

Mari-Luci Antuna. That's me, the middle child.

I'm the one who adored my father and his Mexican heritage, even though we did not see him very much. When I was young, it was not popular to claim your Mexican culture. Most northern New Mexicans identified as Spanish-American. I was different. I loved my Papito's Mexican art, culture, and language. Yes! His Spanish was different from what we spoke in *El Norte*, a term we use to refer to northern New Mexico. At an early age, I embraced the cultures of both Papito and Mamita and learned when to use my two versions of the Spanish language and the traditions that accompanied each of my parents.

I remember an incident when I had to change my use of Spanish. I was on a swing set and I said to one of the kids, *empújame*, in Mexican Spanish. They did not understand me! I then said, *púshame* in Spanglish and finally got the push I wanted. I loved being bi-cultural!

By age ten, I was over five feet tall and very thin. Poor Nanita, she worried that I was too skinny and way too tall for my age. Her constant refrain was, "*¿Cuándo vas a dejar de crecer?*" She would shake her head in amazement and ask when I was going to stop growing. She was 4 feet 6 inches and her height was the measuring stick she used to evaluate my growth.

To make up for my thin frame, Mamita designed dresses for me with puffy sleeves to make my arms look thicker, or inserted a crinoline or petticoat to add volume to my legs. No matter the alterations, she could not hide my lanky frame.

The best quality I did possess was my hair. It was straight, thick, and shiny blue-black in color. I was always stopped on the street by the older girls and asked what I put in my hair to get that shade. I was grateful for my one beauty asset.

I had another characteristic that made me a puzzle to my family. I was a chameleon who could change into a tomboy, a studious reader, or a holier-than-thou little girl within minutes. Totally baffled by me, Mamita would say, "*No se te entiende.*"

Actually no one in my family could figure me out. My problem was I wanted to be everywhere and do everything. I was a leader and a follower. I joined everything, but if I did not like what was happening, I went away and did my own thing. I liked being with people, but also liked playing alone. Dolls, tops, marbles, rope jumping, embroidering, reading the Spanish newspaper, writing stories, working in the garden, playing with friends, racing barefoot, riding horses, chasing skunks…everything was an adventure to me.

I loved nature and all the beauty it brought us. I was forever picking flowers and learned to beautifully arrange them as did Mamita. I was also Nanita's helper in placing little bottles with flowers in her "holy" places all over the ranch. What beautiful colors and how great they smelled. I loved all kinds of plants and their flowers, and I knew most of them by name.

Another pastime I enjoyed during those wonderful summers at my *abuelos' ranchito* was doing what I considered "grownup things." Even when I was a tiny child, I worked very hard imitating adults at work or play. I could not grow up fast enough. By the time I was six, I could sweep the large expanse of ground in front of the house that we called the *patio* as well as anyone in my family. I often swept inside the entire house too. Nanita and Mamita were my models and I tried to learn all that I could from observing them at work. With a little help from them, I mastered many home activities, including making beds that were taut and beautiful to the eye.

Praying out loud to myself was another activity I learned from Nanita and performed on a daily basis. I quickly memorized many prayers and learned to sing the beautiful hymns from the Spanish church prayer books. I really thought I was grown up now. In addition to all these activities, I spent hours reading Catholic stories from Nanita's other books. How I loved to read – whatever the topic – just like my Papito.

Looking after my brother was what I called grownup work. I enjoyed cooing over him and leading him (he did not need much of that) around the house, and even outside if we had permission. I was a regular second mother to him. If he fell, I was good at making his hurt go away by pretending to blow the pain away. I would imitate Mamita and sing, "*Sana, sana, colita de rana. Si no sanas ahora, sanarás mañana.*" Heal, heal little frog. If you don't heal now, you will heal tomorrow. This little sing-song would help him get over his bump or bruise quickly. If it was too bad, we both ran to Nanita who was really a good doctor. I was just in the learning stage, but I must admit I was queasy at the sight of a mere drop of blood. If there was lots of blood, I would tremble, cry to high heaven and look like I was ready to faint. Sometimes people would think I was the one injured.

As I neared my twelfth birthday, I became more studious and wanted to be the very best student that ever existed. That was a lofty goal, but I planned to reach it. I was always with a book in my hand, memorizing everything I read in either English or Spanish. I was no longer called by my nicknames of "Tute," "Tuti," "Luci," "Lucecita," or even *Chírola*, meadowlark. I was now known as Mari-Luci and could not waste any time. I was almost grown up and happily on my way to being somebody. I was not sure what that would be, but I knew that if I worked hard enough, I would not fail.

For some reason, when I was young I dreamed of becoming a secretary in Latin America. I don't know why a secretary. I couldn't even type. And why Latin America? It must have been my Papito's influence. Much later, when I was appointed as the U.S. Ambassador to Honduras, I went to share my good news with my family in Las Vegas. Mamita was the first to congratulate me and said, "*Mijita, se te cumplió tu deseo.*" She was right – I had achieved my dream!

NANITA

Nanita is where I got my zest for life.

My grandmother was a fair-skinned, broad-hipped, tiny beauty. What really set her apart were her big, dark brown eyes and her expressive eyebrows. If she was shocked, or pretended to be shocked, her eyebrows would shoot straight up her forehead. But if she was angry, her eyebrows came tightly together almost forming one single brow. We practiced moving our eyebrows like her, but we never could replicate her dramatic emotions.

My Nanita always appeared stylish, regardless of the work at hand. She would wear a white Peter Pan collar on both her everyday dress and her more elegant ones. She crocheted the collars or made them from cloth with crocheted edgings. On Sundays or party days, she wore a big brooch pinned at her throat. Nanita would even wear a starch-ironed cotton dress and apron when plowing the field with two large horses kicking up tons of dust on her pretty attire. Even though she did hard physical labor, she always wore shoes with a two-inch heel. She claimed shoes with low heels hurt her calves. She seemed so out of place chopping wood or plowing fields in high heels, but I never saw her without them.

Nanita's hair was as neat as her dress. She wore her hair in tight curls created from curlers that she made from the rims of tin-plated coffee cans. She would take the thin strips that came off the lids and cut them into four-inch lengths. She then carefully sewed a small cloth sleeve to fit the strips. Nanita would next roll her wet hair around the covered strips and bend the ends to hold her wrapped hair in place. Nanita rolled her hair every night before going to bed, so she would have ringlets in the morning.

To protect her lovely hairdo when working on the *ranchito*, Nanita wore her *papalina*, a heavily starched and beautifully ironed sunbonnet. When she went to town to visit friends or go to church, she would wear one of four stylish hats: a navy blue or a black straw hat for summer, and a navy blue or a black felt hat for winter. But her hats never looked the same from one week to the other. Every Saturday afternoon, she would redesign a hat by removing whatever decorations were on it and adding something new such as a little piece of veil, a pretty silk flower, a feather, or a few beads. Nanita's hats were always in style and looked new. She got many compliments on them from her *comadres*, who always wore the same old tired ones or a *tápalo*, the traditional black shawl. To me the stylish hats made Nanita look much younger than her friends.

When not busy with work or her clothing, Nanita could be found reciting the *rosario*. She said one *rosario* upon rising, another before bedtime, and many prayers in-between. She claimed that her strength came from a deep faith that the Lord would take care of everyone's problems, but her pious nature that masked her natural playfulness did not fool anyone. Nanita was a bundle of energy and ready to do whatever needed to be done. She gardened, cooked, sewed, cleaned the house, helped her husband on the *ranchito*, took care of her extended family, and nurtured the neighbors and friends who were in and out of her house all day long. Nanita did all these things with exuberance and a deep trust in God.

While Nanita was clearly a very religious lady, I swear she was a northern New Mexican version of Annie Oakley. She never hesitated to use her rifle on the *ranchito*. We children were terribly impressed that she was such a good shot and wondered where and when she acquired the skill.

Nanita sometimes killed magpies because those beautiful black and white little devils would steal the eggs she used to feed her family. Whenever she saw them getting near the chicken coop, she quickly would run to get her gun. She would stand at the edge of the porch and wait until the magpies were strutting around within her sight before she took deadly aim. She was small and when the rifle would go off, she sort of lost her balance and teetered just a bit. Getting herself under control, she would place the gun against the wall, pick up a shovel, and start muttering as she picked up the bird to bury it near the arroyo, *"Esas urracas dañinas tanto que molestan,"* She found those nasty magpies very annoying.

The neighbors talked about how the hawks carried off their chickens and young chicks, although they thought they were beautiful and breathtaking when they rode the air currents. But Nanita disliked the many hawks that stalked her chickens, even more than she disliked the magpies.

Early one morning she spotted a hawk circling her hen house, *rodeando su gallinero*, as Nanita would say. They always circled the coop before coming down for the kill. Nanita ran for her rifle in the house, came outside and stood in her favorite shooting spot to wait for a good shot. As the big hawk flew up into the big blue cloudless sky with Nanita's favorite black hen in its claws, she yelled, "*¡Gavilán malvado!*" calling the sparrow hawk evil.

She then aimed and shot the hawk which was now flying over the field directly across the arroyo. All of us, including Nanita, ran to see if we could find the birds. Soon we found them in the tall weeds. The hawk was deader than dead. The poor chicken, although alive, could not stand up and kept falling every time it tried to take a step. Her neck had been stretched and this severely affected her sense of balance.

Nanita gathered it in her arms, cooing to her beautiful prized hen, as she put it into the coop. The poor chicken was seriously hurt and would not drink or eat. Not wincing, Nanita prepared to kill the chicken. She tied a string around the chicken's feet before placing its neck on the chopping block, swung the axe and with one blow cut off its head. The headless chicken moved around a little before Nanita picked it up. She had a tub of boiling water nearby and before we knew it, she had plucked it clean. It was no big deal. Just one more activity in her busy day. That night Nanita served the family tasty chicken soup with lots of pieces of corn on the cob, green vegetables, and a little rice. Nanita never wasted a thing.

One year she tried raising a few turkeys. She found that the turkeys, however, were pretty dumb and did not repeat that project. During the year she experimented with them, we ate lots of turkey. As soon as they were plump, they got the swinging axe.

On St. John the Baptist's Day, June 24th, Nanita always renewed her baptismal vows by going for a bath in the cold river at four in the morning. While she was gone, Rampo and Mamita would come wake and help us get dressed. They did not want us to miss a single celebration. As Nanita would come up the path and be close to the house, we would belt out the Spanish birthday song, *"Qué linda está la mañana…,"* which starts by recognizing the beauty of the morning.

Nanita would be so happy, she would give us all a hug and get us wet with her long dripping hair. She shivered from the cold bath, so we would hug her tight to try to get her warm. The date actually was her saint's day, not her birthday. She was born on July 28th, but her saint's day was the date she celebrated both her baptism into the Catholic church and her birthday. By five o'clock in the morning, we all were busy in the kitchen making a large breakfast. Of course, the Victrola was playing full blast on the front porch. We were a happy lot early in the morning on St. John's Day and never needed an excuse for dancing.

Nanita completed only two years of elementary school, but she could read and write in her native Spanish. When Nanita was not working, she would read prayer books written in Spanish. Some were about the lives of the saints. With these books, she taught me to read in Spanish before I went to school. She had done the same for my sister years before. When she bought or received an occasional new book, she would always write her name on the first page. She signed them, "Mrs. Juanita R. de Tafoya." She liked that "Mrs.," which let me know she knew more English than she admitted!

While she spoke primarily in Spanish, Nanita was not afraid to speak in English even though she mangled every word she spoke. She would pick up an English newspaper and read it by pronouncing every word phonetically using the Spanish alphabet. As garbled as it sounded, she understood everything she read and would translate it back to us in Spanish.

Once we learned enough English, we would try to correct her, but to no avail. She claimed she could not pronounce the word even when she was saying it correctly. If she saw a robin, she would call it a *robinsón*. We would tell her it was a robin and to say it that way. She would insist on her inability to say the word, insisting, "*No puedo decir "robin", es un robinsón.*"

A family who lived near us in town was named Groth, but she insisted on calling them, Los Grutes. A neighbor child was "Jimmy," but she called him Jimes. My grandpa became Rampo as she decided that is what we would call him instead of grandfather or grandpa in English or *abuelo* in Spanish. *¡Ay! Mi Nanita.* She was a woman with spirit!

Rampo

Rampo was my pillar.

I remember him as 5 feet 10 inches tall, broad-shouldered, and slim-hipped. He had light chestnut brown wavy hair, large bright blue eyes, and fair skin with rosy cheeks just like Nanita. From years of working on the *ranchito*, Rampo's face was heavily weathered, but he was almost always smiling. He seemed so satisfied with his lot in life.

Rampo typically wore large faded blue bib coveralls over beige working pants that he held up with green suspenders. His long-sleeved work shirt was usually also beige. In the winter, Rampo would remove his coveralls on the front porch before going into the house. As I watched him, I could sometimes see the sleeve cuff of his Long Johns peeking out from under his shirtsleeve. During the winter, I saw his Long Johns many times nearly frozen solid and flapping on the clothesline. I never saw Papito undress and seeing Rampo's Long Johns seemed so intimate.

During the summer, he wore much lighter underwear, but most of the time it was still long-sleeved. The underwear, usually beige or light gray, was very visible on the clothesline. His working clothes were finished off with tall gray cotton socks and high-topped, thick-soled, black working shoes.

Rampo also wore a sweat-stained beige colored hat when working in the fields. He never did wear a hat indoors. Men could not enter the house with a hat on because that was a sign of disrespect for the household. When indoors, his hair was always neatly combed with a side part.

In addition, Rampo owned a navy-blue business suit usually worn with a heavily starched white shirt and a dark black tie. He wore this outfit to church on Sundays, holy days of obligation, and for funerals. It was also his outfit for the many dances, *fiestas*, and parties he and Nanita attended.

Rampo attended only a few years of elementary school, but, like many men of his era, he was a self-taught and studied all he could. He spoke fairly decent English and not so badly accented that he couldn't be understood. His Spanish, on the other hand, was flawless when speaking, reading, and writing. On top of his language skills, Rampo had a beautiful orator's voice and did extremely well as a public speaker. His voice was melodious, strong, and deep. In fact, some people called him, *La Lengua de Plata*, the Silver Tongue.

When Rampo spoke, people listened because he also had something interesting to say. He read several newspapers, both in English and in Spanish. Moreover, he always read the *Farmers' Almanac* and a couple of monthly periodicals that he kept near his chair. Because he was an avid reader, his conversations were peppered with ideas not locally known.

He had the manners of a true gentleman and was appreciated for his politeness. When greeting someone, he tipped his hat and was genuinely attentive to all, young or old.

I need to mention that he was a marvelous listener too. Some years after having moved to the *ranchito* in Las Manuelitas, he decided to enter politics. He admired President Roosevelt and The New Deal. Both offered opportunities to improve the living conditions for his family and his *vecinos*. Because he was concerned about his neighbors and had good ideas about helping the poor, he used his good oratory skills to win two elections in the county system, including one as a county judge. These positions gave Rampo a very small but steady income. When he lost, the family simply did without.

Rampo liked music too and taught himself to read sheet music and to play the clarinet quite well. He often entertained us in the evening with his beautiful music while sitting on that great front porch. He sometimes even played in some of Papito's musical groups in nearby towns.

He seemed to be a little bit before his time when it came to ecology. Ecologists weren't well known back then, but Rampo was very aware of the interactions of all creatures in his environment. Vera recalls that one time, as she was walking with him, she was carrying and swinging a long stick. When they passed an ant-hill, she took her stick, poked it into the hole, and tried to disrupt the ants as much as she could. Rampo never said a word and kept on walking.

That evening after prayers, when everyone was quiet and reflective, Rampo told my sister to sit near him. He wanted to find out what the ants did to bother her. He asked, "*¿Qué te hicieron las hormigas para molestarte?*"

She shook her head, saying, "*Nada.*" He explained that the tiny ants had worked very hard to build their little home, and that everyone needed to protect them. My sister and the rest of us understood the great lesson perfectly well.

As young kids running through the lush, green meadows, we often would tear off the flowers and seed pods from the tall plants as we rushed by. But Rampo carefully explained that if we did that, there would be no more flowers. And worse yet, there would be no more plants because the seeds had been destroyed. He understood the meaning of the need for a natural balance in our environment very well.

Our Rampo was an extremely patient man who loved everyone, including us three rascals who were never still. On days when we were particularly troublesome, Mamita would complain to him. He would look up from where he was reading to see what the matter was, oblivious to the ruckus we were causing. When he read, his glasses were perched on the tip of his nose. But when he heard the complaint, he would lower his head in such a way that he could peer over his glasses and, with a twinkle in his eyes, tell us, "*¡Hijitos! Estense quietos. Si no, mañana les voy a tener que pegar.*" How humorous it seems now that Rampo would call us to be quiet and then threaten to spank us – tomorrow! That was our Rampo.

Although Junior and I enjoyed the rainstorms that were accompanied by lightning and loud thunder, Vera did not. She simply was petrified. When the sounds started, she did not know where to hide. Once I heard Rampo tell her that all that noise from above was just God cleaning out his house. God was just like our Nanita, he said. He makes lots of noise shaking rugs, scrubbing pots and pans, and sweeping the dust and dirt out of the house, even slamming the screen door. The explanation seemed to help calm her for a few minutes, but only until the next storm.

One afternoon, the three of us children were squabbling despite the efforts of Mamita and Nanita to quiet us down. Rampo, however, had an idea. In the middle of the boisterous activity, he said, "*Les voy a dar a cada uno su propiedad. Así, no están uno sobre el otro. Por eso están peleando tanto.*" In order to stop us from squabbling, he found a way to keep us out of each other's way. He asked us each to go out and look for a small area that we could call our own. After a long while of searching, up and down gullies, hills, fields, and bushy areas, we returned and told him the spaces we wanted. Vera had chosen a grassy spot near the *río*, surrounded by tall willows. It was a pretty enclosure that looked like a small room. I chose the area under a huge oak tree where I could see all the comings and goings. I never wanted to miss a thing. Junior, all of nine years old, chose the space between two strong trees up on the small *mesa* behind the house. He then asked for a piece of canvas and some rope, and proceeded to make himself a hammock on his "own" property with a view of the entire *ranchito*. He was so darned smart. That activity settled the squabbling and allowed us to pass the time away in our own special places – at least for a while.

We did not have access to many books and magazines until each one of us was old enough to borrow books at the library. Rampo encouraged the three of us to get well educated by reading as much as possible once our chores were done. He would tell us to study hard and get real smart.

Like Nanita, Rampo was a very religious man. He prayed daily. In the early morning he would go up the hillside to where he had erected a huge white cross, made of two thick round logs. He would kneel on the ground for a few minutes and then sit a little longer admiring the beautiful open spaces where he was. At mealtimes, he always led the blessings. In the evening, he was an active participant in the night prayers, which were led by Nanita.

Rampo was an integral part of our young lives. He shared his deep respect for all living things and for his way of life. He was affectionate, and I felt so loved by him, especially when he held us in his arms. Lucky me!

Los Compadres y Las Comadres

Having *compadres* and *comadres* was how we embraced our community.

You could count on Nanita to murmur to no one in particular, "*Vale mas hacer café. Parece que viene mi comadre.*" She immediately would go to the stove and start making coffee. Apparently, she saw her *comadre* coming up the narrow winding path from an adjoining ranch.

I knew we would be in for a treat as eating was the fun part of *comadres* coming to visit. There were always simple, but delicious snacks served during the visits. Sometimes Nanita would tell me to pull out a few *biscochitos*, traditional New Mexican cookies, from the large coffee can where she kept them neatly covered with a sparkling white kitchen towel. I'd smell the cinnamon waft from the can as I opened it and looked forward to eating this crisp, sugary cookie.

After I arranged several *biscochitos* on the plate in a pretty circle, I would walk gingerly with the prized possessions to where Nanita and her *comadre* would be sitting at the kitchen table. In the meantime, Nanita fussed with the fire in the stove. She added water to the coffee pot that already had used *cunques* in the bottom. Then she added a handful of fresh grounds. Coffee was expensive, and everyone tried to make it go a long way. Once the coffee was piping hot, Nanita would pour it into cups; the *comadre* would blow into her cup before taking a drink and appreciatively say, "*¡Ay! Qué bueno y qué caliente.*"

When the used grounds filled the pot to nearly half, Nanita would tell us to throw them out in the garden where they would become fertilizer for our beautiful flowers. Nothing, but nothing, was ever wasted!

When a *comadre* visited, there was always much hugging and kissing and catching up with family news. When they finally sat down to drink coffee, the *comadres* would exchange news about the community. Through this network, Nanita knew everything, even who had gotten drunk, who was having marital problems, and which teenagers were starting to misbehave. Nanita would tsk, tsk upon hearing some of the stories.

The practice of accepting to be a *compadre* or a *comadre* was such an easy way to extend your family by leaps and bounds. Women could become *comadres* by agreeing to do certain things, usually of a religious nature. For example, a woman would become a *comadre* when she agreed to be the sponsor at a baptism or confirmation, or she became a *comadre* when she served as a sponsor at a wedding. Any of these ceremonies entitled one to the title of *comadre*. The same was true for men who became a *compadre* or couples who became *compadres*. Couples might become *compadres* when their children married. The entire two extended families of the bride and groom would bond and create a special relationship. In essence, a bride and groom married a family, not just each other. They all became blood relatives and were now responsible to help each other when times were tough and during special times, to share in family celebrations.

A woman also became a *comadre* if she was asked to take a statue of a saint or a rosary to be blessed by the priest. After the blessing, her family and the requesting family were forever *comadres*, and a new family tie was established. When you were with others at any social gathering and anyone asked why you were *comadres*, you always recited how and what you had done to earn that distinction. Much pleasure, laughter, and gaiety surrounded the explanations.

Over time, *comadres* became sisters. The women would hug each other and tell everyone how much they loved each other. When the wives called themselves *comadres*, many times the husbands became *compadres* and that started the special family relationship.

My *abuelos* had dozens of *compadres* and *comadres*, and we children were encouraged to call them *tíos y tías*, and their children *primos*. Although we came from a very small, nuclear family, we were most fortunate because we had tons of relatives through what we called the *compadrazgo* system.

Everywhere we went in the community, we were recognized as related to someone they knew and were treated with special kindness. The sponsors, or *compadres*, were then the *padrinos* of the participant in the ceremony. All the children of both families became brothers and sisters; your family grew by leaps and bounds.

Because my Papito was not Catholic, Mamita often did not participate as a *madrina* or *comadre* and came up with an excuse for not being able to accept the sponsorship.

However, on occasion she was asked to confirm a girl child and gained a goddaughter, an *haijada*, as we would say in northern New Mexico. Papito never came to understand the deeper meaning of *comadres* and *compadres*. He could not shake the religious aspect of the system and only frowned upon anything related to the church.

Mamita was not deterred. Through sheer determination and due to her strong faith, she managed to have us all baptized and gained three sets of *compadres*. With the *comadres* and *compadres* acquired by Nanita and Rampo and our own three sets, our lives were enriched with friends and family who cared about us as children and, later in our lives, as adults. We were blessed!

Family Photographs

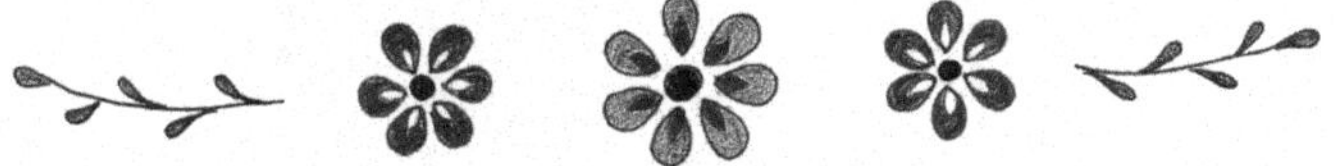

c.1900; Las Vegas, NM: Leonidas Gallegos and Sanjil Ruiz, my biological grandparents, pose for their wedding photograph.

c.1904; Las Vegas, NM: Leonidas Gallegos and Sanjil Ruiz pose with one of their many daughters.

c.1910; Las Vegas, NM: Silviano Tafoya (Rampo) and Juanita Ruiz Tafoya (Nanita) pose with their adopted daughter, Elvira Ruiz (my Mamita).

c.1920; Las Vegas, NM: Elvira Ruiz (my Mamita) married Maurilio Antuna (my Papito), who sits on the arm of her chair. Standing are the best man (Zenon Trujillo) and maid of honor (Maria Trujillo).

My Papito, Maurilio Antuna, had many outfits and talents.

c.1925; Las Vegas, NM: Papito stands to the far right with Tio Ignacio Baca to his left. The other men are likely from the Las Vegas community.

c.1925; Las Vegas, New Mexico: In his shoe shop, Papito stands to the right of Salvador Fernandez (or Hernandez). The person in the background is unknown.

1929; Las Manuelitas, NM. Nanita holds Mari-Luci (age 1), and Vera (age 8) sits beside them, next to the chicken coop.

We enjoyed outdoor fiestas!

c. 1929; Las Manuelitas, NM: Vera poses with a group of *comadres* in front of the rose bushes. Nanita is on the far left, and Mamita is third from the left.

c. 1930-1940; Las Manuelitas, NM: At the *ranchito*. Rampo sits (left) with Uncle Ignacio Baca and Papito on guitar (right).

c. early 1900s; Las Manuelitas, NM: During the summer I watched men on horses playing *El Gallo* during *fiestas.*

1933; Las Vegas, NM: Vera (age 12) puts her arms around Junior (age 3) and Mari-Luci (age 5).

1938; Las Vegas, NM: Mari-Luci (age 10) is with her cousin, Julia Trujillo (same age), who is celebrating her First Holy Communion.

1940; Las Vegas, NM: Junior (age 10) poses with Mari-Luci (age 12).

c.1941; Las Manuelitas, NM: Nanita kneels next to the cross Rampo built up the hill from their *ranchito*.

c.1941; Las Manuelitas, NM: Rampo stands at the front door of his ranch house.

c.1930-1940; Las Manuelitas, NM: Rampo poses beside his Ford. Papito is seated.

1948; Las Vegas, NM: On leave from military training, Junior, now called Bud (age 18), hugs Mari-Luci on the left (age 20) and Vera on the right (age 27).

Photos are courtesy of the National Hispanic Cultural Center, Mari-Luci Jaramillo Collection, MSS0001.

Acknowledgements

This book was fifteen years in the making. After I published *Madame Ambassador: the Shoemaker's Daughter*, many people wanted to know more about my childhood and how it influenced my life. It was my sister, Vera, who encouraged me to share my childhood memories. We both agreed that the visits to our grandparents' small ranch in northern New Mexico were the most memorable.

However, life and a career interfered and writing my childhood memories did not get done. Many decades later, I attempted getting my memories on paper and was thrilled to discover that I remembered many vivid stories of my life between the ages of eight and twelve. I decided right then to put on paper how I felt, who I met, and what I observed during those tender years. I did not intend to offer a historical narrative or novel of these events. I just wanted to share the experiences that, in retrospect, had the greatest influence on my life.

Since I never learned to type very well, I wrote in pencil. One day I showed the stories to a friend, Barbara McCormick, and she typed a few of the narratives. She encouraged me to keep writing, but then she became ill and could no longer help.

Another friend, Joy Dow typed and edited a few more of my hand-written stories and encouraged me to turn them into a novel. While my stories depicted my transition years from being a child to a teenager, I definitely did not have the flair for writing fiction. So, the additional stories were stored away along with my other typed memoirs.

Several years passed again until I had the good fortune of encountering one of my former undergraduate students, now Dr. Cecilia J. Navarrete. In 2016, Cecilia joined a committee of friends to help in establishing the U.S. Ambassador Mari-Luci Jaramillo Endowed Scholarship at the University of New Mexico. The purpose of this scholarship is to assist doctoral graduate students in continuing my vision for creating social justice and education equity for Latinos across the United States. I shared my stories with Cecilia, and she encouraged me to publish them so we could support the Jaramillo Scholarship. Over many months, Cecilia probed my memory for more details, researched the history of my community to fill in gaps, urged me to include the northern New Mexico Spanish I spoke as a child, and helped to organize my stories into a book. Cecilia then applied her artistic talent to illustrate the book we now call *Sacred Seeds*. I am immensely grateful.

I wish to express my gratitude to Susan Durón, Bill Helwig, and Marjorie Rupert for their feedback and edits of an earlier draft of *Sacred Seeds*.

Cecilia and I also thank our spouses, James Elliott and Ron Beauchamp, for their patience and support throughout this project.

Finally, I would like to express my great appreciation to Lisa María Noudehou at Barranca Press for her belief in *Sacred Seeds*, her edits in both languages, and her time and talent in getting the book published.

About the Author: A notable educator and civil rights advocate, **Mari-Luci Jaramillo** is best known as the U.S. Ambassador to Honduras in the 1970s. From humble beginnings in Las Vegas, New Mexico, Mari-Luci went on to a long career that included numerous positions at the University of New Mexico, and serving as the Pentagon's U.S. Deputy Assistant Secretary of State for Inter-American Affairs under President Carter, and as Deputy Assistant Secretary for Latin America under President Clinton. Dr. Jaramillo is the author of *Madame Ambassador: the Shoemaker's Daughter* and resides in Albuquerque.

Co-Author Cecilia J. Navarrete studied under Dr. Jaramillo at the University of New Mexico. She holds degrees from UNM and Stanford University. Dr. Navarrete served 44 years with school districts, state departments, and institutions of higher education, designing and evaluating programs to improve the education conditions of diverse and under-served populations. She resides in Albuquerque.

All proceeds from the sale
of this book benefit the
U.S. Ambassador Mari-Luci Jaramillo
Endowed Scholarship at the
University of New Mexico.

Illustrated
Coming of Age Stories
for ages 12 and up.

CPSIA information can be obtained
at www.ICGtesting.com
Printed in the USA
BVHW071326190819
556214BV00006B/693/P